D1430948

For the Common Good

For the Common Good

Principles of

American

Academic Freedom

MATTHEW W. FINKIN AND ROBERT C. POST

Yale University Press

New Haven & London

Published with assistance from the Louis Stern Memorial Fund.

Designed by James J. Johnson and
set in Melior Roman types by The Composing Room of Michigan, Inc.
Printed in the United States of America.

Library of Congress Cataloging-in-Publication Data
Finkin, Matthew W.
For the common good : principles of American academic freedom /
Matthew W. Finkin and Robert C. Post.
p. cm.
Includes bibliographical references and index.
ISBN 978-0-300-14354-6 (cloth : alk. paper)
1. Academic freedom—United States.
I. Post, Robert, 1947– II. Title.
KF4242.F56 2009
344.73′078—dc22
2008038669

A catalogue record for this book is available from the British Library.

This paper meets the requirements of ANSI/NISO Z39.48-1992
(Permanence of Paper). It contains 30 percent postconsumer waste
(PCW) and is certified by the Forest Stewardship Council (FSC).

10 9 8 7 6 5 4 3 2 1

To all who have defended academic freedom,
especially at great personal cost

Institutions of higher education are conducted for the common good and not to further the interest of either the individual teacher or the institution as a whole. The common good depends upon the free search for truth and its free exposition.

—1940 *Statement of Principles on Academic Freedom and Tenure*

Contents

Introduction

Why This Book?

The American conception of academic freedom crystallized nearly a century ago in the *Declaration of Principles on Academic Freedom and Academic Tenure* created in 1915 by the American Association of University Professors (AAUP). It received its canonical formulation in 1940 in the jointly formulated *Statement of Principles on Academic Freedom and Tenure,* which is presently endorsed by over two hundred organizations. For the past century, American principles of academic freedom have been systematically elaborated and applied in the judicial and legislative work of Committee A—the Committee on Academic Freedom and Tenure of the AAUP. There is by now a small library of scholarly commentary on the subject. Why, then, offer yet another volume of interpretation?

Every generation must earn its own commitments, and the ideals of academic freedom are no exception. In the past decade, frequent and fierce debates about the nature of academic freedom have resulted from a systematic and sustained effort to discipline what some regard as an out-of-control liberal professoriat. These disputes call upon us to determine what academic freedom means in the twenty-first century. They require us to articulate once again the foundational principles that should guide us in explicating the content of American academic freedom.

The current climate of controversy is exemplified by the outrage that erupted in 2003 when the University of North Carolina assigned Barbara Ehrenreich's *Nickel and Dimed: On (Not) Getting By in America* as required reading for incoming freshmen. It has become increasingly ordinary for universities to assign incoming students "common reading" to offer the new freshman class "a shared experience" that might "bring the diversity of student viewpoints to the fore and provide an occasion for modeling the intellectual engagement with different ideas that is expected in college."[1] The University of North Carolina began the practice in 1999 when it chose for discussion Alex Kotlowitz's *There Are No Children Here.*[2] In 2003 the university selected *Nickel and Dimed* and was immediately attacked by the Committee for a Better Carolina, which charged that the university had abandoned "intellectual honesty in favor of [a] political agenda."[3]

The committee denounced the book as a "classic Marxist rant" that mounted "an all-out assault on Christians, conservatives and capitalism." It blasted Ehrenreich as "a self-proclaimed atheist" and a "radical socialist." It criticized the author's "extremist socialist views" and attacked her morals. It adduced statistical evidence to show how well-off America's "poor" really were, faulting Ehrenreich for "declaring that more government and labor unions will solve the problems facing those at the bottom of the income bracket" and for failing to "mention that lack of marriage, high taxes and alcohol, tobacco and drug use could factor into the financial well-being of low-wage workers." The protests of the committee prompted seven North Carolina legislators to visit Chapel Hill to charge the university with creating "an anti-conservative class environment."[4] The legislators objected to "what they thought was the university's attempt to indoctrinate students with leftist ideology."[5] State senator Austin Allran even "asked for the political affiliation of the nine members of the committee that ultimately chose the Ehrenreich book. 'We're for diversity,' Allran said. 'Since the state is about half and half, according to voting patterns, we'd want the committee [to reflect that split].'"[6]

Much of this might sound familiar to the authors of the 1915 *Declaration,* who had insisted that scholars be free to criticize existing social pieties, especially laissez-faire economics. In that year, for example, the Board of Trustees of the Wharton School of the University of Pennsylvania ignored the recommendation of its faculty and refused to renew the appointment of assistant instructor Scott Nearing. Nearing was a prominent Socialist whose teaching had provoked one trustee (active in securing Nearing's removal) to publish a letter in the *Alumni Register* expressing sentiments that were shopworn even at the time: "Joseph Wharton founded the Wharton School of the University to train men for business. It is unfair that teachers benefited by his generous endowment should forget the directions he gave for carrying out the purpose of his gift. Much of the good he aimed at for students and the public is lost when men holding teaching positions in the Wharton School introduce there doctrines wholly at variance with those of its founder and go before the public as members of the Wharton School faculty and representatives of the University, to talk wildly and in a manner entirely inconsistent with Mr. Wharton's well-known views and in defiance of the conservative opinions of men of affairs."[7]

The Committee for a Better Carolina, unlike the trustees of Wharton, did not govern the university, so the committee was not inclined to adopt the simple position that those who pay for higher education ought to control its content. Not even the North Carolina legislators went that far.[8] Instead, the committee and its legislative allies appealed to what they claimed were fundamental principles of university governance. They argued that the assignment of Ehrenreich's book without the concomitant assignment of competing points of view violated scholarly ideals of "balance and fairness" and contradicted the "diversity of thought" that ought to characterize instruction in universities and colleges. At the end of its advertisement opposing the Ehrenreich volume, the committee proclaimed: "*Education, not Indoctrination!*"[9]

In recent years, these themes have been vigorously and loudly reiterated throughout the country. The thought is that a liberal professoriat has subverted and betrayed basic academic values. Universities have substituted partisanship for balance.[10] They have created a "hostile environment" for students with conservative political ideas or Christian religious beliefs.[11] They have undertaken to indoctrinate rather than educate their students.

Never mind the alarming absence of empirical evidence underlying these repeated charges.[12] Our concern in this volume is that these allegations represent a striking new turn in the American saga of academic freedom. Whereas in the early twentieth century debate turned on the question whether academic freedom should exist,[13] contemporary controversies assume the desirability of academic freedom and attempt to spell out its implications. Debate has been joined over the question of what academic freedom does and does not require. We have been moved to write this book because we want that debate to proceed on the basis of a common understanding of the history and structure of American academic freedom.

In our view, American principles of academic freedom have become a victim of their own success. At the end of the nineteenth century, academic freedom was a fighting cause for the American professoriat. American faculty were forced to think carefully about the meaning of academic freedom because they were struggling to make academic freedom a reality. By the end of the twentieth century, however, with the standards of the 1940 *Statement of Principles on Academic Freedom and Tenure* safely incorporated into virtually all institutional policies, academic freedom had slipped from consciousness and become merely a "folkway,"[14] a warm and vaguely fuzzy privilege assumed by faculty as a "God-given right"[15] without careful attention to its hard requirements and logical implications.[16] For too many members of the American scholarly community, academic freedom has become a hortatory ideal without conceptual clarity or precision.

We offer this book in the hope that we can articulate basic principles of American academic freedom that can guide us through current controversies with intellectual integrity and coherence. We return to the original ideals that animated the drafters of the 1915 *Declaration* and explore how these ideals have been applied to the exigencies of the twentieth century. We appeal to texts that have scarcely made an appearance in contemporary debate. Since 1915, Committee A of the AAUP has systematically developed the principles of the 1915 *Declaration* by applying them to the circumstances of concrete cases. Its decisions have been carefully reasoned and have largely adhered to the rule-of-law discipline of stare decisis. Taken together, these decisions provide a rich and useful common law of academic freedom. Because this common law is virtually unknown outside the AAUP, and because it deserves wider dissemination, we draw on it extensively in an effort to clarify essential ideas of American academic freedom.

We begin in chapter 1 by briefly developing the intellectual roots of academic freedom and by demonstrating its internal connections to emerging needs for knowledge and intellectual mastery. Chapter 2 sketches the codification of specifically American principles of academic freedom in the 1915 *Declaration* and the institutionalization of these principles in the review process of Committee A. We argue that the concept of academic freedom proposed by the 1915 *Declaration* differs fundamentally from the individual First Amendment rights that present themselves so vividly to the contemporary mind. The profession's claim to academic freedom is grounded firmly in a substantive account of the purposes of higher education and in the special conditions necessary for faculty to fulfill those purposes. In essence, academic freedom consists of the freedom to pursue the scholarly profession according to the standards of that profession.

Academic freedom is conventionally understood as having four distinct dimensions: freedom of research and publication, freedom in the classroom, freedom of intramural speech, and freedom of extramural speech. Each of these aspects of academic freedom has its own internal logic, and each poses its own conceptual difficulties. Each merits separate consideration, and we therefore examine in chapters 3–6 these four essential attributes of academic freedom.

Taken together, these dimensions of academic freedom express what has become a consensus vision of the purposes of American higher education. Universities and colleges are autonomous professional institutions dedicated to creating new knowledge and to educating young adults to think for themselves. As we emphasize in our conclusion in chapter 7, the drafters of the 1915 *Declaration* feared a "concentrated public opinion" that would undermine the autonomy of higher education through the eco-

nomic power of public and private donors.[17] The draftsmen of the 1915 *Declaration* sought to establish principles
of academic freedom capable of ensuring that colleges and
universities would remain accountable to professional
standards rather than politically or financially beholden to
public opinion. They hoped to construct institutions of
higher education as instruments of the common good
rather than as organizations promoting the private views of
wealthy donors or the passionate commitments of tran-
sient political majorities. Modern debates have once more
put this vision into question. As the enterprise of higher
education becomes ever more dependent on public and
private support, the threat to the public mission envi-
sioned in the 1915 *Declaration* looms larger than ever. We
dedicate this volume to the clarification and advancement
of that mission.

A few initial caveats are in order. We do not in this volume discuss the question of constitutional academic freedom. The constitutional law of academic freedom developed in the United States during the 1950s in response to
efforts to eliminate subversives from the American professoriat. The constitutional law of academic freedom appeals to the First Amendment as a restriction on the capacity of governments to regulate universities and as a
constraint on the authority of state universities to control
their faculty. The constitutional law of academic freedom
has developed along its own idiosyncratic path, and it has
been much affected by specific and local issues of constitutional jurisprudence.[18] In this volume, we address *professional understandings* of academic freedom, rather than

the *constitutional law* of academic freedom. We discuss how all colleges and universities, whether public or private, ought to govern themselves.[19] We do not consider the institution of tenure, which in the public mind is the idea most closely associated with the AAUP. Since 1940, the AAUP has promulgated many procedural requirements that, like tenure, it regards as necessary to protect the values of academic freedom. Debate about these requirements, like debate about tenure,[20] presupposes a firm grasp of the underlying values that make up academic freedom. Our focus in this short volume is on the nature of these fundamental values, not on the procedures that may be necessary to instantiate them.

CHAPTER 1

The Historical Origins of the Concept of Academic Freedom

Academic freedom first appeared as a distinct concept in the late eighteenth century, though it spoke German at the time. German thinkers drew from the wellspring of the Enlightenment, which in turn drew from even deeper currents in intellectual history.

Throughout civilized human existence there have been ideas that cannot be expressed, questions that cannot be asked lest civil or ecclesiastical authority be offended or threatened.[1] Let us begin with the stark impulse to suppress. It is visible in the book of Exodus. Tradition has it that when Korah led his rebellion against Moses, Korah questioned the law Moses had given the people, which required them to put blue fringes on the corners of their garments and to put a portion of the law on a scroll attached to the doorpost (a mezuzah).

As Louis Ginzberg recounts the story, Korah and his company appeared before Moses clothed all in blue. Korah asked Moses if they were then required to attach blue fringes, to which Moses responded that they must.

> "If," replied Korah, "one fringe of [blue] suffices to fulfill this commandment, should not a whole garment of [blue] answer the requirements of the law, even if there be no special fringe of [blue] in the corners?" "Must a Mezuzah be attached to the doorpost of a house filled with the sacred Books?" Moses answered, "Yea." Then Korah said: "The two hundred and seventy sections of the Torah are not sufficient, whereas the two sections attached to the door-post suffice!" . . . "Laws so irrational," said Korah, "cannot possibly trace their origin from God. The Torah that thou didst teach to Israel is not therefore God's work, but thy work, hence art thou no prophet."[2]

These questions might well be put to a class by a professor of theology or law today, but the response given at the time was, not to put too fine a point on it, biblical: the earth was made to swallow Korah and his followers.

Just as there has always been an impulse to suppress, so there has always been an instinct to resist. We find no advocate of academic freedom claiming kinship with Korah whose purpose in questioning authority was to foment political rebellion rather than to search for truth. But by the late nineteenth century several historical figures were customarily invoked as martyrs in the cause of intellectual freedom. Socrates typically heads the list, which invariably also includes Galileo. Giordano Bruno is often mentioned as well. Socrates has been much discussed, as has Galileo.[3] So let us turn instead to the Campo de' Fiori (the Field of Flowers) in Rome, where, on February 17, 1600, Giordano Bruno, his jaws sealed by iron spikes lest he give public voice to yet more heresy, was burned to death.[4]

It was not Bruno's physics but his metaphysics that brought him to the attention of the Inquisition, though one should not discount Bruno's maddeningly vexatious personality.[5] In response to the sentence passed upon him, Bruno replied to his judges, "Perhaps your fear in passing this sentence upon me is greater than mine in accepting it." Unlike Galileo, whose confrontation with the church opens to modernity and to the triumphant epistemology of science, Bruno posed an older challenge. He obstinately and vehemently defended the right to think, write, and teach. Bruno stood for the freedom of philosophy to contend with the established truths of theology.

In 1588, Bruno had published in Prague the *Articuli centum et sexaginta adversus huius tempestatis mathematicos atque philosophos,* a book whose dedication to Emperor Rudolph II exudes the individualism and self-confidence of Jacob Burkhardt's Renaissance. It is worth noting at length. "Now as all this concerns the freedom to teach [*Quod vero ad liberas disciplinas attinet*]," Bruno wrote,

may I keep at arm's length not only the habit of belief, instilled in me through the teachings of tutors and parents, but also that "common sense" which—in many circumstances and places (as far as I have been able to judge for myself)—seems to engender deceit and distortion; may I keep them so at arm's length that I never assert anything, in the field of philosophy, without reflection or without grounds; and, for me, may all things remain equally open to doubt whenever they come up for discussion, whether they are things generally acknowledged to be abstruse and absurd, or whether they are things considered to be among the most certain and the most evident. Indeed, when debating ideas, it is harmful to define something without first weighing well its meaning; it is wicked to nod agreement out of exaggerated respect for others; it is mercenary, servile, and contrary to the dignity of the freedom of Man to bend the knee to another in unquestioning devotion; it is rank stupidity to believe out of habit; it is irrational to echo the opinion of the majority, as if the number of wise men must necessarily exceed or equal or approximate the infinite number of fools, or as if such a great multitude (even if they all blindly accepted the authority of Aristotle, or another leader of the same sort), could, while stumbling and lumbering forward in the darkness, understand or be worth more than, or even as much as, someone who has chosen to decide for himself.[6]

Though Bruno was charged by the Inquisition with eight counts of heresy on the basis of statements extracted from his published works, one commentator concludes that he was burned less for any of these in particular than for "his wanton *curiositas,* for his belief in the limitless capacity of man to know—to know, eventually, what God knows."[7] In the middle ages, *curiositas* alone was grounds for accusa-

tion. Those guilty of it were, in J. M. M. H. Thijssen's felic-
itous phrase, "victims of a curious mind."[8]

Consider the case of Noël Journet, who in 1582 was
burned to death in France for "blasphemy and execrable
atheism."[9] Journet, a twenty-eight-year-old former soldier
—pockmarked, redheaded, and of average stature[10]—
teacher to the children of the village of Sainte Raffine, had
learned a smattering of German and Flemish but not much
else. He had been baptized a Catholic, converted to the Re-
formed Church, and proceeded to scandalize both. He attacked the authenticity of scripture largely on the ground
of inconsistency and incredibility: How could Moses have
written the five books if he describes his own death and
burial in it? How could Samson bring down a building
with his bare hands? Either the columns were architec-
turally far too close or his arms were inhumanly long. How
could Sarah, at her age, possibly kindle the pharaoh's lust?
And a good deal more. He concluded that all of it, Chris-
tianity included, was a fraud. His books were burned along
with him, and Henry III congratulated the magistrates on
their diligence.

Journet's trial occurred at a critical juncture, when elite
attitudes toward the acquisition of knowledge were beginning to evolve. The medieval church had been critical not
only of the pride of knowledge but also of the desire to
know things not useful to salvation, of *curiositas.* The idea
of forbidden knowledge continued to exert influence in
the sixteenth century, in religious as well as in cosmic and
political matters. Paul's words in Romans 11:20—"be not
high-minded, but fear"—were mistranslated and applied

to condemn knowledge itself. In 1507 an Italian translator put it, "non volere sapere le chose alte—that is, do not seek to know high things."[11] But about the time of Journet, the idea of *curiosity* was in the process of changing.[12] The concept of desirable knowledge was beginning to take root, working, as Carlo Ginzburg has illustrated, a literal reversal of values.

Instead of "altum sapere periculosum (it is dangerous to know high things)" displayed in conjunction with an illustration of Icarus's fall in an emblem book of 1618, a plate of 1686 shows Icarus in flight accompanied by the motto "Nil linquere inausum (Dare everything)." In 1719, Antoni van Leeuwenhoek, the first to use a microscope for zoological study, adorned the title page of his *Letters to the English Royal Society* with the motto "Dum audes, ardua vinces ("if you will dare, you will overcome every difficulty)."[13] At the end of the century Kant asked, What is enlightenment? and he answered in terms that echo Giordano Bruno: "*Sapere aude!* Have courage to use your *own* understanding!"[14]

This change was heavily influenced by the rise of science, the emergence of a desire to collect, categorize, test, and reproduce by public demonstrations and performances, to hear presentations, and to disseminate results. Science, as J. Robert Oppenheimer remarked, pushes toward the articulation of "standards for giving meaning to questions and to discovering whether we are in agreement about what we are talking about."[15] Science foregrounds the inevitability of "human fallibility" and the consequent need for critical reexamination.

The development of commerce was also enormously influential. Note, for example, the change in cartography. "Medieval cartographers," Marcia Colish tells us, "were not interested in displaying the period's geographical knowledge with scientific precision or to scale. Maps, for them, had a didactic and spiritual value; they placed Jerusalem at the center of the earth's surface because of its perceived spiritual centrality."[16] By the eighteenth century, however, merchants, governments, and the military required maps crafted with practical precision.

An analogous "intellectual transformation" in the assembly, display, and understanding of information worked its way throughout society.[17] As the need for specialized information expanded, so did the need for the expertise to collect, collate, and interpret information.[18] "The steady growth of commerce," David Fellman explains, "led to the emergence of a philosophy of knowledge which stressed the basic contingency of ideas, and the utility of testing the value of ideas, not in terms of the power of those who espoused them, but rather in terms of their capacity to stand up under the competition of other ideas. There was a logical transition from the competition of the marketplace to the competition of ideas."[19]

As a consequence of these developments, the intellectual landscape of Bruno and Journet fundamentally changed. There emerged the possibility of questioning received truths and institutions.[20] Publishing his *Historical and Critical Dictionary* in 1692, Pierre Bayle, like Journet, also insisted on the Bible's inconsistencies, but Bayle survived to write a good deal more. "Evidently," Anthony

Grafton writes, "something had happened in the intervening century. An exegetical as well as scientific revolution had taken place."[21]

These developments were foundational for the establishment of academic freedom. The exile of Christian Wolff, a professor of mathematics and physics at the University of Halle who was reputed to be among the most distinguished philosophers of natural law and ethics in all of Europe, can serve as a figurative turning point. In 1723, King Frederick William I of Prussia himself ordered Wolff's banishment: "And hereby We also make known and declare, by Our Most Gracious order, that the aforementioned Professor Wolff be no longer permitted to remain here, and be not allowed to teach; and furthermore, the said Wolff be duly notified that within forty-eight hours after the reception of this order he is to depart the city of Halle and all our other royal dominions under pain of the halter [that is, the gallows]."[22]

The king acted at the prompting of two Pietist generals who had been petitioned by members of the theology faculty at Halle to sanction Wolff's theological teachings, which were, they stressed, outside his license to teach mathematics. (Wolff was a popular teacher whose students had developed the disquieting propensity of challenging theologians in the classroom to prove their assertions.) The king acted not to punish Wolff's lack of teaching authority but because his generals had advised him that Wolff's theological determinism would increase military desertions. Wolff's position on predetermination of human action seemed to imply that desertion was a matter over which individual soldiers had no control and bore no moral responsibility. This was not a proposition that the soldier-king could regard with equanimity.

Wolff's expulsion triggered a polemical explosion throughout Europe. More than two hundred tracts addressed the case, most defending Wolff in terms of the "freedom of philosophy."[23] In honor of Christian Wolff, Count Ernst Christoph von Manteuffel founded the *Societas Alethophilorum* (Society of the Friends of Truth) in 1736. A medal was struck bearing the legend from Horace *sapere aude!* (dare to know!). Intellectual freedom was taken to have prevailed when the new king, Frederick II (Frederick the Great), restored Wolff to Halle in 1740 as professor of public law and mathematics, vice chancellor of the university, and Prussian privy councillor (*Geheimer Rat*). The "triumph of the Enlightenment in Prussia" was complete when Wolff was made an imperial baron (*Reichsfreiherr*) in 1745.[24] A half century later the philosopher Johann Gottlieb Fichte could proclaim that "free investigation of every possible object of thought is without doubt a human right."[25] As rector of the University of Jena, Fichte addressed the subject of "*akademische Freiheit*" (academic freedom) in 1811, by which time the term had already begun to take on a life of its own.[26]

The term invoked an important but subtle affiliation with the idea of the medieval university. The privilege of scholars to study controversial texts and to essay novel propositions of philosophy and theology had been asserted since the fourteenth century. But as J. M. M. H. Thijssen explains in the context of the controversies at the

University of Paris, the medieval concept of these privileges included neither freedom of teaching nor freedom of learning per se, but was based instead "on the principle of the freedom of the academic institution to manage its own affairs."[27] In medieval thought, institutional autonomy was linked to the perceived integrity of reason and scholarly expertise. Thijssen emphasizes that "viewing medieval academic censures solely in terms of restrictions on academic freedom or the imprisonment of reason . . . misses the distinct *rational* aspect in the process of examining and censuring medieval academics. Academic heresies and errors were demonstrated in a process of rational discourse, by cognitive criteria that were provided by experts."[28]

However much a bishop might demand hierarchical respect for his office, he could not require deference to his theological reasoning. The Cistercian theologian Peter of Ceffons professed to have witnessed profound subtlety "silenced as error by a judge into whose head 'subtlety would have entered as easily as a fully loaded elephant could get through a finger ring.'"[29] An enduring contribution of the medieval university can be found in the demand that judgments of scholarly competence belong to a body of scholarly masters. This idea of academic expertise as a collegial prerogative underwrote the institutional autonomy of the university and could be invoked to counter the dictates of nonacademic authority.

Medieval freedom of rational inquiry was nevertheless bounded on the one side by the limits of what the church was prepared to condemn as heresy and on the other by the distinction between scholarly disputation among experts and inciting doubt among the unlettered. The doctoral oath at the University of Wittenberg, which Martin Luther swore in 1512, granted a doctor of theology unhindered freedom to discuss questions of scriptural interpretation short of disseminating heretical doctrine; the Wittenberg faculty specifically extended this freedom in 1518 to Martin Luther's ninety-five theses.[30] But Cardinal Cajetan, conducting the only official interrogation the church was able to make of Luther, raised the distinct question of free publication and concluded: "Although Brother Martin has put his opinions in the form of theses for academic disputation, he has nonetheless put them forward as firm results in sermons, and even, as I have been told, in the German language—within earshot of everyone, even the common 'stupid people.'"[31] Medieval freedom of academic disputation did not extend to freedom of public address, least of all in the vernacular.[32]

By the eighteenth century, prohibitions against heresy and public disputation were crumbling before new attitudes toward knowledge. German and Swiss universities could assert the traditional independence of the university, founded on the collective expertise of its masters, without these ancient limitations. These universities embraced the ideal of *Wissenschaft,* which, as Walter Metzger points out, does not translate accurately as "science." In fact, no English noun quite captures it. To Metzger, *Wissenschaft* meant "a dedicated, sanctified pursuit . . . the morally imperative study of things for themselves and for their ultimate meanings."[33] To David Hollinger, it carries a sharper meaning: "The truths sought by *Wissenschaft* were discovered, not divined. Excluded were truths one might claim on the basis of religious experience, poetic insight, speculation, common sense, or practical but undisciplined experience in the workaday world."[34] *Wissenschaft* required, as Fichte asserted in 1811, academic freedom (*akademische Freiheit*), which entailed both autonomy for the university as a self-governing body and freedom of teaching and learning. A cantonal law of Zurich of September 28, 1832, provided: "In higher learning academic teaching and learning freedom is established [*An der Hochschule gilt akademische Lehr- und Lernfreyheit*]."[35] Bern followed suit in 1834.

The movement toward academic freedom in Germany was uneven. Political repression continued in some German states after the Congress of Vienna. The "Göttingen Seven," led by Professor Friedrich Christoph Dahlmann, were dismissed for refusing to swear allegiance to a new, less liberal constitution. "If [*Wissenschaft*] is no longer permitted to have a conscience here," Dahlmann wrote, "so must it seek another home."[36] In 1841, August Heinrich Hoffman von Fallersleben, who wrote "Deutschland über Alles," the anthem of German unification, was summarily dismissed from a professorship at Breslau for writing political songs that displeased the authorities in violation, as the order of dismissal explained, of his obligations as a public official.

By the time of German unification, *akademische Freiheit* was taken as a defining condition for higher education, virtually as a matter of course. Upon assuming the rectorship of the University of Berlin in 1877, Hermann von Helmholtz proclaimed in his speech on academic freedom in German universities that "the extreme consequences of materialism in metaphysics, [and] the fearless speculation on the basis of Darwinian evolutionary theory are unhindered [here] as is even the most extreme idolization of papal infallibility."[37] In 1930, Abraham Flexner observed wistfully that a German professor was "perfectly free in the choice of topics, in the manner of presentation, in the formation of his seminar, in his way of life. Neither the faculty nor the ministry supervises him: he has the dignity that surrounds a man who, holding an intellectual post, is under no one's orders."[38]

The American concept of academic freedom grew directly out of the German concept of *akademische Freiheit.* As the second half of the nineteenth century began, American higher education was dominated by colleges that were small, regionally or locally based, and predominantly denominational. The curriculum tended to be classical; the educational mission centered on the building of "character" more than the nurturing of scholarship. The professoriat derived heavily from clerical backgrounds; appointment was often a way station for the young who were awaiting a clerical call or, for the old, a relief from penury. As Christopher Jencks and David Riesman put it, "Until the late nineteenth century there had hardly been an academic profession at all."[39]

After the Civil War, Americans of academic aspiration increasingly chafed at the lack of serious scholarship and sought study abroad. A significant number made the pilgrimage to Germany. They returned impressed by the German model and imbued with the concept of an institution committed to the ideal of *Wissenschaft* and to its concomitant freedom of research and teaching. Local institutions, eager for national recognition, sought these young Ph.D.'s, who, in turn, reshaped American institutions and contributed to the professionalization of the American professoriat. Beginning with Johns Hopkins University in 1876, Americans began to create institutions based on the German model.

When rising American academics sought to transplant *akademische Freiheit* to America, they confronted an organization of higher education very different from that which existed in Germany. Universities in the United States were not under the independent control of faculty. They were instead governed by a lay board chosen by a private proprietor, by a sponsoring religious denomination, or by a political process. The chief officer of the American university was a president who was selected by and accountable to a lay governing board. German universities, following the ancient medieval model of a self-governing collection of masters, lacked a governing board, an office of president, and elaborate administrative structures. The German university confronted an external structure of bureaucratic control. In American institutions, by contrast, the "outside was ensconced within."[40] Uniquely in American universities, therefore, faculty were considered employees of an institution that was controlled by a nonprofessional governing board. Because faculty, like all employees, served at the will of their employers, it seemed to follow that in America nonscholars retained the right to decide what should and should not be taught, what should and should not be published.

In 1902, no less a figure than Alton B. Parker, chief judge of the New York Court of Appeals, president of the National Civic Federation, and a candidate for the U.S. presidency, argued for the "rights of donors" in rebuttal to the emerging claim of academic freedom: "And as to the founders of, and donors to, institutions of learning, whose sole business in life—money-making—may not have especially qualified them to determine what should be taught in colleges and universities, I am in favor of their having the like complete freedom within their province which I accord to teachers within theirs—freedom to insist upon it that the doctrines they believe to be true, and for the propagation of which they have expressly and avowedly founded the institution, or endowed the chairs, shall be taught in such institutions."[41] Parker insisted on the autonomy of the university, but in Parker's view autonomy was vested in the donors and trustees, not in the faculty.

Controversies were not long in coming. In 1878, only months after Helmholtz extolled the freedom to propound Darwinism at the University of Berlin, Alexander Winchell was dismissed as a professor of geology at Vanderbilt University by its president, Bishop McTyeire, because Winchell's views on evolution were taken by people of influence to be "contrary to the 'plan of redemption.'"[42] (Winchell was immediately hired by the University of Michigan and later became president of the Geological Society of America.) The Winchell case prompted Andrew

Dickson White, the founding president of Cornell and the future author of a polemic on religious hostility toward science,[43] to write to Daniel Coit Gilman, the founding president of Johns Hopkins University.

> What an idea of a University those trustees must have! What was tragical in Galileo's case is farcical in this. It appears that Bishop McTyeire took great pains to show Winchell that there was no similarity between the two cases. Neither of them was aware that the Bishop used precisely the same argument to Winchell—indeed, virtually, *verbatim*—which Cardinal Bellarmin used to Galileo. . . . What a theory of a University it is, to be sure; and yet that is what our opponents all over the country seem to be struggling for. Very hard to see that the world progresses any, if, instead of being in the hands of a Roman Catholic Cardinal, we are to fall into the hands of a Methodist Bishop. The real advance is the fact that they have no longer any power to oppose us with physical torture. In view of the spirit shown, and the articles written, against Winchell for his very moderate tendency to evolution doctrines, it would seem that the absence of torture is not due to any lack of will in the matter.[44]

Incident was followed by incident, several attracting considerable notoriety. We might mention William Graham Sumner's dispute with Yale president Noah Porter in 1879 over Sumner's use of Herbert Spencer's *Study of Sociology* as an undergraduate text; the attack on Richard T. Ely for "teaching socialism" at the University of Wisconsin in 1894, which resulted in what was to become a historic endorsement of academic freedom by Wisconsin's board of regents;[45] and the termination of Edward Bemis of the University of Chicago, which is thought to have been based on his critique of the railroads as corrupting the political process.

The result was a rich decades-long public debate that culminated in the formation of the American Association of University Professors and its promulgation in 1915 of the *Declaration of Principles on Academic Freedom and Academic Tenure.*

CHAPTER 2

The 1915 *Declaration* and the American Concept of Academic Freedom

The architects of the American idea of academic freedom were required to adapt the German conception of *akademische Freiheit* to a very different political and institutional setting. German professors were employees of the state and civil servants of high status. Academic freedom did not exempt German professors from the application of a disciplinary code requiring loyalty to the state; nor did it protect them as private citizens from state regulation. The professional autonomy that American graduate students so admired in the late nineteenth century could be conceived of as a compromise in which the state left scholars to their *wissenschaftlich* work so long as they otherwise acted as obedient civil servants.

American professors, by contrast, did not regard themselves as high-ranking bureaucrats. They considered themselves citizens of a democratic republic. If they sometimes worried about professorial participation in partisan politics, it was not because faculty owed an obligation of loyalty to the state but because such participation might threaten "habits of scholarship."[1] American professors sought a version of academic freedom that reflected the influence of "a stronger social and constitutional commitment to the idea of freedom of speech," as well as a more pragmatic commitment to the social utility of professional scholarship.[2] But these differences, critical as they are, should not obscure the essential fact that the American vision of academic freedom, like the German *akademische Freiheit,* derives almost entirely from an understanding of the vocation of scholarship.

The 1915 *Declaration*

The first systematic articulation of the logic and structure of academic freedom in America, and arguably the greatest, was the 1915 *Declaration of Principles on Academic Freedom and Academic Tenure.* Contemporary principles of academic freedom derive directly from the *Declaration,* which was drafted chiefly by the economist Edwin R. A. Seligman and the philosopher Arthur O. Lovejoy,[3] both of whom were intimately acquainted with and appalled by the fact that American professors were deemed at law to be employees subject to the plenary control of their employers.

Seligman and Lovejoy had each been witnesses to the notorious dismissal of the economist Edward A. Ross in

1900. Advocating for free silver and against the importation of cheap Asian labor, Ross had so profoundly distressed the co-founder and proprietor of Stanford University, Mrs. Leland Stanford, that she wrote the university's president, David Starr Jordan: "I must confess I am weary of Professor Ross, and I think he ought not to be retained at Stanford University. . . . I trust that before the close of this semester Professor Ross will have received notice that he will not be re-engaged for the new year."[4] Jordan obeyed his instructions. Lovejoy was so outraged that he resigned his position at Stanford; Seligman was so offended that he instigated a pathbreaking investigation of the incident by the American Economic Association.

At the very time that they were drafting the 1915 *Declaration,* both Seligman and Lovejoy were involved in the AAUP's investigation of the dismissal of Scott Nearing by the Board of Trustees of the University of Pennsylvania "because it is understood that the Trustees did not approve of some of the doctrines he taught."[5] The trustees gave no explanation for Nearing's peremptory removal.[6] Reflecting the American legal doctrine of employment at will, the *New York Times* opined in response to the resulting furor that "trustees are not obliged to give reasons for dismissal."[7] At law, employers could, in the absence of contractual restraints, "discharge or retain" employees "for good cause, for no cause or even for cause morally wrong, without thereby being guilty of a legal wrong."[8] As employees, faculty were subject to this "arbitrary power of dismissal."[9] When the University of Pennsylvania trustee George Wharton Pepper was asked to explain Nearing's firing, he replied: "If I was dissatisfied with my secretary for anything he had done, some people might be in favor of my calling him in here and to sit down and talk it over. Others might think it wiser to dismiss him without assigning any cause. But in any case I would be within my rights in terminating his employment."[10]

The lesson was not lost on the American professoriat. Trustees "have legal authority to employ and dismiss whomsoever they wish in the service of their institution—the President, the professors, administrative officers, janitors, and day laborers. And no one of these, it is well to note, has any more constitutional security of tenure than another. They can discharge a janitor who complains that his wages are low, or an instructor who makes the fact known to his classes."[11] This allocation of authority was justified, the *New York Times* explained, because

men who through toil and ability have got together money enough to endow universities or professors' chairs, do not generally have it in mind that their money should be spent for the dissemination of the dogmas of Socialism or in teaching ingenuous youth how to live without work. Yet when Trustees conscientiously endeavor to carry out the purposes of the founder by taking proper measures to prevent that misuse of the endowment, we always hear a loud howl about academic freedom.

We see no reason why the upholders of academic freedom in that sense should not establish a university of their own. Let them provide the funds, erect the buildings, lay out the campus, and then make a requisition on the padded cells of Bedlam for their teaching staff. Nobody would interfere with the full freedom of the professors. They could teach Socialism and shiftlessness until Doomsday without restraint.[12]

The first and foremost task of those who sought to protect academic freedom was to alter this idea that faculty were employees serving at the mere sufferance of their employers, a notion that, as John Dewey wrote in a letter to the *New York Times,* was "based upon the conception of the relation of a factory employer to his employe[e]."[13] The radical nature of academic freedom cannot now be grasped unless we first appreciate the way in which academic freedom would seem "peculiar chiefly in that the teacher is in his economic status a salaried employee, and that the freedom claimed for him implies a denial of the right of those who provide or administer the funds from which he is paid, to control the content of his teaching. The principle of academic freedom is thus, from a purely economic point of view, a paradoxical one; it asserts that those who buy a certain service may not . . . prescribe the nature of the service to be rendered."[14]

The 1915 *Declaration* confronts this paradox head on. It attacks the "conception of a university as an ordinary business venture, and of academic teaching as a purely private employment." Faculty, it asserts, "are the appointees, but not in any proper sense the employees," of universities.

Once appointed, the scholar has professional functions to perform in which the appointing authorities have neither competency nor moral right to intervene. The responsibility of the university teacher is primarily to the public itself, and to the judgment of his own profession; and while, with respect to certain external conditions of his vocation, he accepts a responsibility to the authorities of the institution in which he serves, in the essentials of his professional activity his duty is to the wider public to which the institution itself is morally amenable. So far as the university teacher's independence of thought and utterance is concerned— though not in other regards—the relationship of professor to trustees may be compared to that between judges of the federal courts and the executive who appoints them. University teachers should be understood to be, with respect to the conclusions reached and expressed by them, no more subject to the control of the trustees than are the judges subject to the control of the president with respect to their decisions; while of course, for the same reason, trustees are no more to be held responsible for, or to be presumed to agree with, the opinions or utterances of professors than the president can be assumed to approve of all the legal reasonings of the courts.

The core principle of American academic freedom may be found in this remarkable passage. It argues that faculty are not "employees" answerable to the will of their employers but instead "appointees" responsible "to the wider public" for the fulfillment of the social function of universities.[15] The 1915 *Declaration* justifies the transformation of faculty from employees to appointees on the basis of two key conceptual premises. The first concerns the purpose of the university as an institution; the second concerns the professional expertise of faculty.

The *Declaration* asserts that an essential objective of the university is "to promote inquiry and advance the sum of human knowledge." What constitutes true knowledge is not to be determined by the private views of individuals, even those individuals who happen to own universities. Knowledge is the result of the public disciplinary practices of professional experts. Because faculty are professional experts trained in the mastery of these disciplinary practices, they are "appointed" to discharge the essential university function of producing knowledge. In this task they are answerable to the public at large rather than to the particular desires of employers.[16]

The *Declaration* asserts that academic freedom is necessary if universities are to accomplish their mission of advancing "the sum of human knowledge." "The first condition of progress," the *Declaration* declares, "is complete and unlimited freedom to pursue inquiry and publish its results. Such freedom is the breath in the nostrils of all scientific activity." It follows that "the university teacher's independence of thought and utterance" is required by the basic purpose of the university. As Lovejoy later succinctly put it, the university's "function of seeking new truths will sometimes mean . . . the undermining of widely or generally accepted beliefs. It is rendered impossible if the work of the investigator is shackled by the requirement that his conclusions shall never seriously deviate either from generally accepted beliefs or from those accepted by the persons, private or official, through whom society provides the means for the maintenance of universities. . . .

Academic freedom is, then, a prerequisite condition to the proper prosecution, in an organized and adequately endowed manner, of scientific inquiry."[17]

The *Declaration* acknowledges the existence of institutions of higher education that call themselves "universities" but that are actually dedicated to propagating a particular vision of the truth, as, for example, when "a wealthy manufacturer establishes a special school in a university in order to teach, among other things, the advantages of a protective tariff." But the *Declaration* insists that such organizations should be considered "essentially proprietary institutions" that do not "accept the principles of freedom of inquiry, of opinion, and of teaching. . . . Their purpose is not to advance knowledge by the unrestricted research and unfettered discussion of impartial investigators, but rather to subsidize the promotion of opinions held by the persons, usually not of the scholar's calling, who provide the funds for their maintenance." It is "manifestly important," the *Declaration* asserts, that such institutions "not be permitted to sail under false colors. . . . Any university which lays restrictions upon the intellectual freedom of its professors proclaims itself a proprietary institution, and should be so described whenever it makes a general appeal for funds; and the public should be advised that the institution has no claim whatever to general support or regard."[18]

The *Declaration* directly confronts university trustees who conceive "the relation of trustees to professors . . . to be analogous to that of a private employer to his employees; in which, therefore, trustees are not regarded as debarred by any moral restrictions, beyond their own sense of expediency, from imposing their personal opinions upon the teaching of the institution, or even from employing the power of dismissal to gratify their private antipathies or resentments." Such trustees, the *Declaration* charges, do not understand "the full implications of the distinction between private proprietorship and [the] public trust" entailed by a proper account of the social function of the modern university.[19] They fail fundamentally to appreciate that true universities serve the common good by producing knowledge and that the production of knowledge requires freedom of inquiry.

The second conceptual premise of the 1915 *Declaration* is that faculty are professional experts in the production of knowledge. This premise might today be thought controversial in some circles.[20] The *Declaration* presupposes not only that knowledge, however provisional, exists and is articulable, but also that knowledge is advanced through the free application of highly professionalized forms of inquiry.[21] The *Declaration* claims that universities can advance the sum of human knowledge only if they employ persons who are experts in their disciplines and only if universities liberate these experts to apply freely the disciplinary methods established by their training. Although this claim seems most obviously defensible in the context of scientific inquiry, it retains its force whenever we believe that a discipline's methods produce knowledge, as, for example, we plainly do in the social sciences and humanities.

The implication of this perspective, however, is that the "liberty of the scholar within the university to set forth his conclusions, be they what they may, is conditioned by their being conclusions gained by a scholar's method and held in a scholar's spirit; that is to say, they must be the fruits of competent and patient and sincere inquiry." Here the *Declaration* echoes Hermann von Helmholtz's 1877 address on academic freedom at the University of Berlin. Scholars must be free to debate any academically controverted matter so long as the debate is *wissenschaftlich*—so long, that is, as the discussion proceeds on the basis of scholarly standards.[22]

The Distinction between Academic Freedom and Freedom of Speech

The *Declaration* conceives of academic freedom not as an individual right to be free from any and all constraint but instead as the freedom to pursue the "scholar's profession" according to the standards of that profession. Academic freedom consists in the freedom of mind, inquiry, and expression necessary for proper performance of professional obligations. Because regulation may be necessary to ensure that scholars comply with the requirements of the "scholar's method," the *Declaration* necessarily and explicitly repudiates the position "that academic freedom implies that individual teachers should be exempt from all restraints as to the matter or manner of their utterances, either within or without the university."

This account of academic freedom explains why universities today routinely require faculty to comply with academic standards.[23] They hire and promote professors on the basis of evaluations that are supposed to reflect the application of professional norms. They distribute grants on a similar basis. Academic departments define the content and ordering of courses and instruction according to these same criteria. It is no exaggeration to say that universities simply could not function if they were deprived of the capacity to apply such standards.

Academic freedom, therefore, does not protect the autonomy of professors to pursue their own individual work free from all university restraints. Instead, academic freedom establishes the liberty necessary to advance knowledge, which is the liberty to practice the scholarly profession. This point is fundamental. Although the First Amendment may prohibit the state from penalizing the *New York Times* for misunderstanding the distinction between astronomy and astrology, no astronomy professor can insulate himself or herself from the adverse consequences of such a conflation.[24] If the First Amendment protects the interests of individual persons to speak as they wish, academic freedom protects the interests of society in having a professoriat that can accomplish its mission. The *Declaration* advances a theory of academic freedom that invokes "not the absolute freedom of utterance of the individual scholar, but the absolute freedom of thought, of inquiry, of discussion and of teaching, of the academic profession."[25]

Professional Self-Regulation

Echoing the legacy of medieval scholars, the *Declaration* insists that professional standards "cannot with safety" be enforced "by bodies not composed of the academic profession." "Lay governing boards are competent to judge concerning charges of habitual neglect of assigned duties, on the part of individual teachers, and concerning charges of grave moral delinquency. But in matters of opinion, and of the utterance of opinion, such boards cannot intervene without destroying, to the extent of their intervention, the essential nature of a university—without converting it from a place dedicated to openness of mind, in which the conclusions expressed are the tested conclusions of trained scholars, into a place barred against the access of new light, and precommitted to the opinions or prejudices of men who have not been set apart or expressly trained for the scholar's duties." Because faculty are "professional scholars" who have received "prolonged and specialized technical training" in the disciplinary expertise necessary to advance knowledge, the *Declaration* is clear that they should be accorded the prerogative of governing themselves.

The *Declaration*'s argument for professional self-regulation rests on two grounds. The first is the privilege of expertise. Lay persons are said to lack the training and skills necessary to apply norms of professional scholarship, which can be acquired only through rigorous study. The second is the need to ensure that the mission of the university to advance knowledge is not impaired by the application of standards other than those of professional scholarship. Because lay persons have not been socialized into the knowledge and practice of professional norms, they will tend to enforce standards or proceed on assumptions that are extrinsic to the profession. The *Declaration* imagines such standards and assumptions as dangerous because they are likely to distort professional norms of inquiry in the service of popular political beliefs (in the case of public universities), in the service of private prejudices (in the case of proprietary universities), or in the service of ecclesiastical dogma (in the case of parochial universities). Lay enforcement of professional norms would thus invite distortions that might well prove incompatible with the basic mission of the university.[26]

On the whole, the professoriat's claim to self-regulation has proved remarkably durable and successful. Other professionals—lawyers, doctors, even the clergy—have had to submit to increasingly pervasive forms of public regulation. But the professional autonomy of faculty remains a powerful and effective fact of university life. This might be because the public, although it cares very much about the actions of doctors and lawyers, is relatively indifferent to the actual practices of universities. But it might also be because the progressive vision articulated by the 1915 *Declaration* remains persuasive. The public may genuinely believe that universities have on the whole successfully fulfilled their function of producing valuable knowledge and that this production would be seriously compromised were universities to circumscribe academic freedom.

Public Support for Academic Freedom

The university's value in producing scientific and technical knowledge, as well as training skilled professionals, is obvious and incalculable, especially in today's information society and knowledge-based economy. Even if the public may sometimes display less regard for the value of knowledge produced by humanities scholarship, academic freedom signifies that the self-regulation of the university is indivisible; it extends to all scholars in the university or to none at all. Academic freedom rests on a covenant struck between the university as an institution and the general public, not on a contract between particular scholars and the general public.

A great strength of the ideal of academic freedom propounded by the 1915 *Declaration* is that it ties the protection of university-wide academic freedom to the production of social goods that the public actually requires. The exchange of freedom for knowledge is a legacy of the eighteenth century, when escalating demands in commerce, government, and the professions for a sophisticated mastery of information and knowledge first became apparent. In the long run, public support for academic freedom will endure as long as the public need for the creation of such knowledge.

Such support would vanish, however, if academic freedom were reconceptualized as an individual right authorizing faculty to research and publish in any manner they personally see fit. This may not be immediately obvious, because we are so accustomed to thinking of individual First Amendment rights as establishing a "marketplace of ideas."[27] But there is no particular reason to believe that unrestrained speech, by itself, will produce knowledge.[28] On any plausible account, the production of knowledge requires not merely the negative liberty to speculate free from censorship but also an affirmative commitment to the virtues of reason, fairness, and accuracy.[29] As the philosopher Bernard Williams reminds us, compliance with these virtues, enforced through social and legal means, is central whenever we witness a sustained dedication to the actual production of knowledge, as, for example, within the practice of organized science.[30]

The traditional ideal of academic freedom, with its twin commitments to freedom of research and to compliance with professional norms, nicely balances these negative and affirmative dimensions. This balance would be lost if academic freedom were reformulated as an individual right that insulates scholars from professional regulation.[31] Reformulated in this way, academic freedom would regard the communication of each scholar as equally protected and thus enforce the premise, explicit within First Amendment doctrine, that there is an "equality of status in the field of ideas."[32] It is clear that this premise is inconsistent with the advancement of knowledge, which requires precisely that ideas be treated unequally, that they be assessed and weighed, accepted and rejected.[33] The kind of individual freedom that underlies the structure of First Amendment rights is for this reason ill suited to the production of knowledge. It instead expresses the postulate of equal, intrinsic, individual dignity that lies at the foundation of legitimacy in a democratic state.

It might be thought that academic freedom exists to protect the distinct value of free and critical inquiry. But great conceptual and practical difficulties arise if we seek to explain academic freedom as an effort to safeguard this value. In a democracy each and every citizen is entitled to enjoy the liberty of free and critical inquiry, and it is therefore unclear why scholars should receive special protections for this liberty, protections that other Americans do not generally possess against their private employers. If faculty claim these special protections by virtue of their rigorous professional training, it must be explained why free and critical inquiry is more valuable to those who have undergone rigorous professional training than to those who have not, especially in light of the claim that academic freedom should immunize scholars from the application of the very professional norms that this training is designed to instill. And if faculty claim these special protections by virtue of their association with universities, it must be explained why scholars, as distinct from other university employees, should enjoy these special protections and why universities, as distinct from other private institutions in a democracy, should be required especially to respect the value of free and critical inquiry.[34]

Academic freedom, if it is do the hard work of protecting faculty from the waves of repression that periodically sweep through the American polity, must explain why scholars ought to enjoy freedoms that other members of the public do not possess. The ideal of academic freedom advanced in the 1915 *Declaration* offers a compact and historically convincing explanation for this disparity. Academic freedom is the price the public must pay in return for the social good of advancing knowledge. It is difficult to see how academic freedom could effectively counter public demands for restrictions on scholarly liberty if academic freedom were reconceived simply as an individual right. Were academic freedom primarily a protection for the value of free and critical inquiry, which is a universal value in a democracy, public control over scholars would seem neither more nor less justifiable than restraints that apply to the public generally.

Codification and Explication

In April 1915, Arthur O. Lovejoy, a professor of philosophy at Johns Hopkins University and a founder and general secretary of the AAUP, read an editorial in the *New York Evening Post* while riding a bus in Manhattan. The editorial called upon the newly born AAUP to investigate the resignation of seventeen faculty members at the University of Utah. Lovejoy proceeded to the home of John Dewey, then AAUP president, who provided rail fare to Utah to look into the matter. Lovejoy traveled straightaway to Salt Lake City and initiated the AAUP's first investigation.[35] The process became a fixture on the academic scene.

In the two-year period 1916–1917, over thirty complaints of alleged infractions of academic freedom were brought to the attention of Committee A, the AAUP's Committee on Academic Freedom and Tenure and the successor to the body that had drafted the 1915 *Declaration*. The committee's reports for that early period outline the procedures it set in place to investigate complaints, which included independent factual inquiry, attempted conciliation, and, in significant cases, investigation by an ad hoc committee of inquiry. The committee report for 1917 explained, "It is difficult to formulate the general rules of academic freedom in such a way that a clear and unmistakable line shall be drawn between the field of utterance which it protects and the field for which it sets up no defenses. . . . Between those cases where dismissal would be a clear and unmistakable infringement of academic freedom and those cases where it is equally clear that the principle of academic freedom cannot be invoked as a defense, there is a narrow and uncertainly mapped area where judgment must hinge upon a knowledge of the background and all the attending conditions of the individual case."[36] It then adverted to the role of the investigations it had undertaken: "They supplement and amplify the general report of 1915 on academic freedom and academic tenure—with which also they are, without exception, in substantial harmony—by contributing to the building up of a body of case law, gradually bringing a larger variety of specific issues under the control of general principles."[37] John Henry Wigmore, a distinguished and hardheaded professor of law at Northwestern University, affirmed in his 1916 AAUP presidential address that the five reports of investigating committees thus far published "are weighty documents, which would do credit to any judicial court in the world; and their findings must convince all readers that no more impartial and competent tribunal could be found for such cases."[38]

In subsequent years the higher-education community began to see the advantages of developing a common statement of governing principles of academic freedom. In 1925, a multiorganizational assemblage convened by the American Council on Education produced a joint conference statement.[39] Its basic conclusions governing academic freedom were later summarized in this way: "(1) A teacher's freedom in investigation may not be restricted except to prevent undue interference with his teaching duties; (2) a teacher shall have full freedom to expound his subject in and out of the classroom, provided he has due regard for the needs of immature students, and, in denominational or proprietary schools, he must adhere to any express agreement, made in advance of his employment, limiting his freedom of instruction; (3) a teacher may not introduce into his class discussions controversial and irrelevant subjects outside his own field of study; (4) a teacher, in his extra-mural utterances, is entitled to the same freedom as any other citizen, but he should make it plain that he is speaking for himself and not for his institution."[40]

These conclusions were conceptually weak and did not receive institutional adoption or administrative endorsement. The AAUP began to search for a negotiating partner for a successor statement. The obvious institution would have been the Association of American Universities,[41] but it was disinclined. The Association of American Colleges, then the leading organization of liberal-arts colleges (with substantial denominational college membership), agreed to enter into negotiations, which commenced in 1936. The resulting document was completed in 1938 and, after modification, was ratified by both organizations in 1940. As Walter Metzger observes, portions of the 1940 *Statement of*

Principles on Academic Freedom and Tenure bear the unmistakable signs of the times and of the professoriat's negotiating partner.[42] It is well to emphasize that the 1940 *Statement* is a compact, a treaty that reflects concessions by both parties.

The 1940 *Statement* has since become the standard of academic freedom in the United States. It is now endorsed by more than two hundred educational organizations and disciplinary societies. It has been adopted by name or in text in innumerable college and university rules and regulations[43] and is frequently cited in court opinions. The 1940 *Statement* provides assurances for the protection of academic freedom, but defines "academic freedom" only in the most general terms. Academic freedom requires "full freedom in research," "freedom in the classroom," and "free[dom] from institutional censorship or discipline" for citizens and "officers" of educational institutions. The 1940 *Statement* throws up a constellation of unanswered questions.

For this reason, the *Statement* provides guidance only as it is interpreted and applied to specific situations. As Committee A's 1947 report observed, the "full meaning" of the 1940 *Statement,* "like the meaning of provisions of the Constitution of the United States, is subject to gradual discovery, by a process analogous to that of judicial inclusion and exclusion, as the principles are applied to case after case. That is to say, the full code of faculty rights and duties is always in process of definition."[44] The task of systematically interpreting and applying the 1940 *Statement* has fallen to Committee A of the AAUP.[45] Committee A both adopts prospective policy, like a legislature,[46] and investigates the facts of concrete complaints and applies pre-existing principles, like a court. Committee A has by now compiled almost a century of case law interpreting and applying the principles of academic freedom and tenure.

The Judicial Process of Committee A

Any faculty member may seek advice from AAUP staff assigned to Committee A. If a faculty member requests that the AAUP take action, the matter is categorized as a "complaint." Further information is usually required and a dossier is compiled. If, on the basis of the information supplied by the complainant, no prima facie departure from AAUP-supported standards (or institutional regulations) is apparent, the matter will be closed. More than half the complaints received by AAUP national staff are usually terminated in this way.

If a complaint appears to be well founded, AAUP staff will seek to discuss it with administrative officers at the complainant's institution. The complaint then ripens into a "case." The case may be resolved if further information supplied by the institution's administration indicates that no significant departure from AAUP-supported standards has occurred. A great number of cases end at this stage of the process. If the case appears to be well founded, however, the national staff will attempt to negotiate a resolution that is acceptable to all sides. Many cases are resolved in this way.[47]

The AAUP general secretary may authorize an official

investigation of cases that prove intractable and that appear to involve significant violations of the principles of the 1940 *Statement*. An investigation begins with the appointment of an ad hoc committee, usually consisting of two or three faculty members selected on the basis of disciplinary expertise, kindred institutional affiliation, and personal competence. The ad hoc committee of investigation receives a dossier and is briefed by AAUP staff, but the committee is free to determine the scope of its own investigation and to reach its own conclusions. The committee visits the campus and attempts to interview all relevant witnesses, including faculty, students, trustees, and alumni.

The committee's report is submitted to the general secretary, who, after editorial discussion with the committee, may submit the report to Committee A for authorization to publish. Committee A evaluates the findings and reasoning of the report.[48] If the report is authorized for publication, a confidential prepublication copy is sent to the principals for comment, primarily to ensure factual accuracy. Some administrations, especially in recent years, have chosen to submit rather lengthy commentary. Where relevant, portions of the response may be noted in the published report; in some recent cases the AAUP has brought the full text of an administration's response to the attention of the academic community via its Web site.

In 1938 the AAUP began to publish a list of administrations censured by vote of the association's annual meeting.[49] Censure is imposed on the basis of investigations published in the year preceding the annual meeting. Committee A reviews these reports and makes a nonbinding recommendation about whether to impose censure. If the annual meeting votes to censure, AAUP staff are required to work with the censured administration in an effort to bring it into accord with the 1940 *Statement* and AAUP principles.[50] Some administrations seek to avoid censure and some seek to have censure removed quickly; but in most cases removal is effected only after a number of years, typically when a new administration takes office and the principals to the event have departed. In the ten-year period 1995–2004, nineteen institutions were placed on the censure list and sixteen were removed; the median duration of listing of the latter was twelve years. The longest, the College of the Ozarks, had been listed for thirty years; the shortest, the University of Southern California, for three.

As Judge J. Skelly Wright observed, the opinions of Committee A reflect merely the conclusions of an "organization composed of professors alone."[51] To the courts, these opinions constitute arguments about the meaning of the 1940 *Statement* that possess only persuasive power. But this view understates their importance to the general field of academic freedom. As the reasoned conclusions of an especially knowledgeable body, the opinions of Committee A offer an unusually rich resource for understanding the meaning of academic freedom in America. They strive to interpret a governing instrument, the 1940 *Statement*, which has achieved near-universal acceptance in the academic community. They do so in a disciplined, lawlike way, seeking to apply principle to context, often by reasoning from precedential analogies.[52] They are guided by a professional staff, drawn largely from the ranks of the professoriat, which serves as a national clearinghouse for questions of academic freedom and which has thus acquired a great breadth of experience. Committee A opinions are reasoned and transparent to the community affected by it. They are backed by a system of sanctions that, although lacking the coercive power of the state, are nevertheless consequential. The opinions thus conduce toward a coherent national system of norms.

As a result, academic freedom has assumed a surprising uniformity of meaning throughout the United States. It does not mean one thing at a small private eastern college and quite another at a large public midwestern university. The legislative elaboration and judicial gloss placed on the 1940 *Statement* by Committee A, a body that has been in continuous existence since 1915, supplies the most authoritative available source for the professional meaning of academic freedom today. We rely on this repository of experience in what follows.

The vast majority of Committee A opinions interpret the various procedural guidelines that the AAUP has from time to time enacted to protect academic freedom. But in this volume we appeal to those few select Committee A judgments that address the fundamental substantive principles of academic freedom we seek to illuminate. These opinions gain in persuasive force by speaking across time to modern circumstances.

CHAPTER 3

Freedom of Research and Publication

The 1940 *Statement* provides that "teachers are entitled to full freedom in research and in the publication of the results, subject to the adequate performance of their other academic duties; but research for pecuniary return should be based upon an understanding with the authorities of the institution."[1] The *Statement* does not use the adjective "full" to describe any other aspect of academic freedom.

The unqualified robustness of the 1940 *Statement*'s assurance for freedom of research and publication harkens back to the 1915 *Declaration*. Walter Metzger has observed that the authors of the 1915 *Declaration* recognized "no such thing as dangerous knowledge; whether there was such a thing as a dangerous way of gaining knowledge, they did not wonder or at least did not ask. . . . Though the great European war had started, shattering the optimism of social philosophers, these Americans had probably not yet grasped the disillusive lessons of the battlefield—that the chemistry that advances human life can also be utilized to destroy it, that the biology that cures disease can also be put into homicidal use."[2]

The 1940 *Statement* lists freedom of research and publication first among the distinct dimensions of academic freedom because this freedom follows most directly from the fundamental mission of the university to create new knowledge. The basic claim is that researchers cannot develop new knowledge unless they are free to inquire and to speculate. They cannot advance knowledge unless they are free to share the results of their research with peers and with the general public. There is today general agreement on these basic principles.

Theoretical Foundations

A deep conceptual difficulty nevertheless lurks at the center of this essential dimension of academic freedom. What the 1915 *Declaration* calls "independence of thought and utterance" can create new knowledge only when exercised within a framework of accepted professional norms that distinguish research that contributes to knowledge from research that does not. It is this framework that connects academic freedom with the function of expanding knowledge. As Edward Shils has observed: "Academic freedom certainly extended to intellectual originality. It was for the departmental colleagues of their own university and their peers outside their own university, when one of them departed from that consensus, to decide whether the individual in question was being original, or divergent within reasonable limits, or eccentric to the point of mental incapacity, or impermissibly arbitrary, indolent, or otherwise irresponsible. Sanctions for their failure to conform with accepted intellectual standards could not be denounced on the grounds that they infringed on the right of academic freedom."[3]

The difficulty is that independence of thought and utterance cannot be so easily cabined. Critical inquiry can turn on the very framework of "accepted intellectual standards" that is supposed to distinguish true knowledge from false belief. An individual scholar can always claim that he or she is developing new and different intellectual standards, and this claim can be justified on the incontestable ground that such standards are themselves forms of knowledge that must be open to critique and development. We are thus led to a paradox. Intellectual standards are required to connect the exercise of academic freedom to the production of knowledge, yet intellectual standards are also themselves forms of knowledge whose evaluation requires academic freedom. Academic freedom thus appears to be dependent on, yet independent of, intellectual standards.

This paradox lies coiled at the core of the traditional justification for freedom of research and publication. It is plainly unacceptable to imagine that professional norms ought to be uniquely immune from criticism and disagreement. Like all forms of knowing, these norms can be improved by the dialogue that flows from independence of thought and utterance. The point is succinctly articulated by Joan Scott: "Disciplinary communities . . . share a common commitment to the autonomous pursuit of understanding, which they both limit and make possible by articulating, contesting, and revising the rules of such pursuits and the standards by which outcomes will be judged. . . . This recognition insists on a place for criticism and critical transformation at the very heart of the conception of a discipline and so guarantees the existence of that scholarly critical function that discipline is meant to legitimate and that academic freedom is designed to protect."[4]

Yet it is plainly unacceptable to believe that professors possess "full freedom" to violate professional norms. Without the discipline of accepted intellectual standards, the very justification for freedom of research and publication is undermined. Academic freedom can no longer claim to produce warranted knowledge. There can be no "equality of status in the field of ideas" within universities, at least within universities as we presently know them.[5] How far, then, does the "full freedom" of research extend?

The dilemma is not quite as sharp as it might at first blush appear. An appreciation of controversy and hence of independence of thought and utterance is built into the very structure of professional academic standards. Contestation drives the conversation that constitutes ordinary scholarly life. Dispute and innovation is propelled by many factors, including naturally arising differences of opinion, competition for prominence and success, the ordinary progression of generations, and, as David Hollinger has shrewdly observed, the fact that "any particular disciplinary community exists within what we might see as a series of concentric circles of accountability in an informal but vitally important structure of authority."

As Hollinger writes, "In order to maintain its standing in the learned world as a whole, a given community must keep the communities nearest to it persuaded that it is behaving responsibly, and it must also, partly through the support of these neighboring communities, diminish whatever skepticism about its operations might arise in more distant parts of the learned world, and beyond, in the society that scientists and scholars do, after all, serve. . . . The farther you get from the technical particulars of the field, the less authority you have to decide what should be going on."[6] Toleration of disagreement, and thus freedom of research and publication, is in this way woven into the everyday practice of scholarship. This toleration extends not only to controversial claims about the substance of knowledge but also to the "accepted intellectual standards" by which such claims should be evaluated.

That having been said, it must also be observed that the content of professional norms involves judgment and interpretation and is for this reason always contestable. It can be quite controversial whether, in any given case, professional norms ought to be interpreted in a manner that tolerates variant forms of scholarly practice. Cases at the frontier of a discipline can grow highly contentious, generating sharp disputes that are not susceptible to definitive theoretical resolution. This has important consequences for the practice of academic freedom. It implies that the institutions of peer review that apply professional standards are perennially vulnerable to suspicion and distrust. They can always be charged with having become merely the self-serving guardians of entrenched forms of academic power.

Unfortunately there are all too many occasions for such charges. Controversies over professional standards are endemic to American universities. "Quantitative versus qualitative, positivist versus metahistorical, Robertsonian versus Lévi-Straussian, realist versus Leo Straussian: the academic life has always been an endless series of turf battles."[7] Especially in the years since the Vietnam War, these battles have proceeded in the general context of a growing "antinomianism"[8] within American intellectual culture that is skeptical of authority and distrusts those who seek to exercise it.

When this antinomianism presses on exactly the most vulnerable point of scholarly self-governance, which is the extent to which faculty ought to have academic freedom to reformulate the very professional norms by which they are to be judged by their peers, the results can be corrosive. This is no doubt an important reason why academic freedom has in recent decades increasingly come to be conceived as an individual right to be asserted against all forms of university regulation, including the constraints of peer review. It is easier and more comfortable to support the conscience of the individual scholar than the potentially abusive authority of an established and corporate faculty who may merely be protecting their own prerogatives and prejudices.

It is worth noting, therefore, that no university currently

deals with its faculty as if academic freedom of research and publication were an individual right to be fully free from all institutional restraint. Universities instead hire, promote, grant tenure to, and support faculty on the basis of criteria of academic merit that purport to apply professional standards. Individual faculty have no right of immunity from such judgments. To reconceive this aspect of academic freedom as an individual right would require not merely developing a new justification for freedom of research and publication, a justification that would not depend on the connection between disciplinary standards and the production of knowledge, but also developing a new and convincing account of pervasive contemporary structures of university governance. No convincing solution to either challenge is currently visible on the horizon.

That is why the actual exercise of academic freedom of research and publication continues to depend on the application of professional norms, even though support for these norms has grown increasingly disenchanted. Although most now acknowledge that it may be impossible definitively to distinguish peer-review processes in which disciplinary standards are properly applied from those in which reviewers improperly engage in professionally self-serving behavior,[9] we may nevertheless have good reasons to encourage institutions of peer review to continue to make the tacit judgments necessary to balance toleration with discipline. Some cases at the margin may be irresolvable, but institutions of peer review nevertheless work well enough to sustain the basic justification for academic freedom of research and publication. Most cases, most of the time, involve what Thomas Kuhn famously called "normal science," the unexceptional application of unexceptional professional norms.[10]

This analysis suggests that the traditional ideal of academic freedom of research and publication is imperiled in at least two distinct ways. The first threat is external. The danger is that the general public will override the prerogatives of faculty self-governance just as they have overridden the ambition for self-regulation of professions like law and medicine. The strongest counter to this external threat is the contention that academic freedom is necessary to produce new knowledge. This has been the profession's major line of defense when attacked.

The defense makes visible a second threat to academic freedom, one that is internal. This threat is skepticism. The external defense of academic freedom will collapse if faculty lose faith in the professional norms necessary to define and generate knowledge. The traditional ideal of freedom of research and publication can be sustained only if those who exercise the prerogative of peer review interpret disciplinary standards in a manner that maintains the internal legitimacy of these standards. The interpretation of these norms will thus predictably and appropriately be influenced by the need to preserve sufficient social cohesion within the profession to sustain the authority of these norms.[11] As a practical matter, successful institutions of peer review will therefore maintain a sensible and wise equilibrium between innovation and stability. The ultimate constraint, however, is whether peer reviewers apply disciplinary norms that over time produce credible forms of knowledge.

A close analysis of academic freedom of research and publication makes visible the dangers inherent in viewing academic freedom as an individual right. An individual-rights account of academic freedom of research and publication would organize peer-review processes on the basis of a professed skepticism of professional norms, and such skepticism would undermine whatever authority these norms might in fact possess. The conception of academic freedom as an individual right seems superficially attractive because it appears to promise greater security for academic dissent, but in the long run it undercuts the professional norms necessary for the external defense of academic freedom.

Freedom of Research

Limits on research and publication have been sought and sometimes secured by corporate sponsors,[12] and government has not infrequently sought to impose restrictions on research and publication to protect governmental interests, especially in the name of national security.[13] Academic freedom in the sense that we are considering it, however, concerns the relationship between faculty and institutions of higher education, not the relationship between faculty and external institutions like the state or corporations. Universities only rarely seek to suppress freedom of research and publication. Committee A precedents on this aspect of academic freedom of research and publication are therefore rare. In this chapter we examine two major cases. The first, which we consider in this section, involves the University of Missouri and concerns freedom of research; the second, which we consider in the following section, involves the University of Montana and concerns freedom of publication.

The case involving the University of Missouri began in 1929, when envelopes were placed in several hundred student mailboxes. The envelopes contained a letter from an organization identifying itself as the "Bureau of Personnel Research" and included a questionnaire that could be returned without postage to a university box. The resulting uproar, which originated with a "petition from townspeople in Columbia" asking "for the removal of the professors and students concerned with the questionnaire,"[14] led to the suspension of Professor Max Meyer, a distinguished member of the faculty with decades of service, and the dismissal of Professor Harmon DeGraff. The AAUP sent an investigating committee.[15]

A recent study of these events by Lawrence Nelson captures the public outcry and the editorial outrage.[16] Nelson places these events in the context of changing sexual mores in the American Midwest in the late 1920s. In considering the case, we ought to resist the temptation to condescend to its quaintly Victorian facts. We ought instead to imagine how we would respond if we received a questionnaire that was as offensive to us as this one was to many Missourians.

The first three questions of the questionnaire, among its most offensive, were

1. (a) If you were engaged to marry a man and suddenly learned that he had at some time indulged in illicit sexual relations, would you break the engagement?

(b) Would you break the engagement if you learned that he had so indulged frequently and indiscriminately?

(c) And if, after marriage, you were to find that your husband was sexually unfaithful to you, would you terminate your relations with him?

2. (a) Would you quit associating with an unmarried woman on learning that she had at some time engaged in sexual irregularities?

(b) On learning that she had so engaged often and promiscuously?

(c) On learning that she had accepted money in return for her sexual favors?

(d) Would you quit associating with a married woman on learning that she had engaged in extra-marital sexual activities?

3. (a) Are your own relations with men restrained most by religious convictions, fear of social disapproval, physical repugnance, fear of pregnancy, lack of opportunity, fear of venereal diseases, or pride in your ability to resist temptation?

(b) During your childhood, did you ever engage in mutual sexual play with another individual?

(c) Since sexual maturity, have you ever engaged in specific sexual relations?[17]

The questionnaire had been prepared by a student, Orval Hobart Mowrer, for Professor DeGraff's course on "The Family." It was to be a class project. Mowrer consulted Professor DeGraff on the questionnaire's construction and circulation. DeGraff, in turn, consulted his senior colleague Professor Meyer on the design and execution of the project.

The president and the executive board of the university's board of curators essentially charged DeGraff and Meyer with two derelictions: that the questionnaire "could not produce any scientifically valid conclusions nor any facts likely to be of substantial value" and that the distribution of the questionnaire harmed students by tending to make them sexually immoral and subjecting them to shock and distress.[18] These charges were sustained by the full board of curators, which explained in its order terminating DeGraff and suspending Meyer that

> whatever else a university may be, it must be a place to which parents may send their children with full confidence that the surrounding moral atmosphere will be sane and wholesome. Fortunately such is now the condition at the University of Missouri. . . .
>
> It is the opinion of the Executive Board that students should not be made subjects of investigation by other students particularly when such investigation by its very nature tends to create the condition which it is alleged to correct.
>
> Neither can we find any justification for any inquiry that from its very nature could not produce any scientifically valid conclusions nor any facts likely to be of substantial value.
>
> We feel that the responsible individuals have a radically mistaken conception of the essential conditions which must prevail in order to establish and maintain public confidence in the University.[19]

The first charge against DeGraff and Meyer asserts the right of a lay board of administration to control the agenda of professional scholarly research. The AAUP investigating committee directly challenged this assertion:

The Board of Curators object to the questionnaire on the basis that "the inquiry from its very nature could not produce any scientifically valid conclusions or any facts likely to be of substantial value." The first question at issue here is whether the Board of Curators is competent to pronounce upon the scientific value of an investigation sponsored by any member of the University faculty. The Committee concedes that the Board can express itself about the social expediency of an investigation and about other such general and public aspects of current scientific work. But it is presumptuous for a Board of Curators to make pronouncements about the scientific value of any investigation. Scientific investigations do proceed in all reputable universities in spite of differences of opinion about their validity. Scientific validity has never been established by any legal procedure or by the dictates of any board. A part of the criticism about scientific validity was based on the fact that undoubtedly some of the answers to the questionnaire would not be truthful. This is a contingency present in all science and especially in social sciences.

One of the principal objects of social science is to study objectively the various social institutions and the factors which cause them to change. An important group of these institutions includes betrothal, marriage, and the family. These social institutions rest largely on a code governing sex conduct. Conduct which complies with this code is called moral. The explicit formulation of this code we call our ideals. If we want to investigate objectively, the ideals that govern people's action in relation to sex, including engagements and marriage, the most obvious procedure is to ask people what their ideals really are with regard to the many forms of sex conduct. It is legitimate to ascertain the consensus of opinion of various social groups about the sex code with its changes, and college students constitute a very large and influential group involved in these social institutions. What they believe is of importance to know, both for social science and for practical life. Hence it seems entirely legitimate to ask the three questions which are in dispute [the first three of the questionnaire].

It is of course admitted that the questionnaire is not so satisfactory a fact-gathering device as the instruments of the older sciences, but it seems to be the most direct and at present almost the only available method of ascertaining what people regard to be right and wrong.

The history of science is repeating itself. The honest inquiries of Galileo about the physical aspects of the universe trespassed on the taboos of his time so that Pope Urban declared that "it is a question of the most godless business which could ever be discussed—that the doctrine was in the highest degree sinful." Charles V, in France, forbade the possession of furnaces and apparatus necessary for chemical processes, and Henry IV did the same in England. . . . Biological science is still fighting for freedom of honest inquiry. The teachings of Linnaeus about sex in plants was for many years prohibited in the papal states and elsewhere in Europe. But in 1773, permission was given that they be discussed in Rome! . . . The investigation and teaching of evolution still trespasses on the taboos of some states. Now social science has its turn so that factual inquiry about the social institutions that are based on our sex code simply must not be made in some parts of the world because they offend the taboos of the generation that is passing.[20]

The AAUP investigating committee responded to the second charge by concluding that "there is little or no evidence that any student receiving the questionnaire was shocked or insulted by it. There is no evidence that the questionnaire led to sexual immorality or to decreased self-control in the matter of sex behavior on the part of the students." The committee explained that "it is . . . clear that the questionnaire could have done no harm or injury to the moral life of the students, unless we assume that focusing the attention of the students on these problems for an hour or a day is injurious to one's morals. The leading students, men and women, appearing before the Committee, were unanimous on the point that the capacity of the questionnaire to arouse eroticism is nothing in comparison to many factors of the environment in normal life."[21]

The real cause of the board's actions was articulated by the university's president, Stratton Duluth Brooks, in his interview with the AAUP investigating committee. The distribution of the questionnaire, he said, was "bound to disturb the opinions of a large number of people."[22] Brooks was of course correct in this diagnosis. An editorial in the *Columbia Daily Tribune* denounced the questionnaire as "filthy, degrading, immoral, revolting, and perverted in character and tone." It announced that "the people of Missouri . . . are decidedly of the opinion that decency, refinement, and gentle breeding are better and finer gauges of what is right and proper than that of so-called scientific research applied by a few visionaries. So the verdict of the folk is: The judgment of the pedagogues be damned."[23] Critics of the questionnaire in the pulpit did not shrink from finding Communism at work.[24] A federal appeals court judge defended the university's president, calling the AAUP report "radically progressive," and spoke of "extremists and zealots in sociology, religion and politics [being let] loose upon students of an impressionable age."[25]

The essential lesson of the University of Missouri case is that the propriety of scientific research must be judged by scientific standards, not by the pieties of public opinion.[26] This is a powerful principle because an outraged public can inflict great damage on the reputation and resources of institutions of higher education. There will always be strong incentives for colleges and universities to suppress research that offends important constituencies. The University of Missouri case stands for the simple but fundamental proposition that offense, outrage, or moral disapproval is not a proper ground for the regulation of research. This proposition, in turn, stands for the importance of ensuring scholarly fidelity to the disciplinary practices that define and constitute knowledge, practices that are not to be confused with mere public displeasure.

Underlying the Missouri case, however, is a deeper problem for which there is no easy or entirely principled solution. Research, like any form of human behavior, can cause harm, and academic freedom is not a license to commit harm. Universities can regulate research to ensure safety, as, for example, when faculty work with dangerous materials like toxins or radioactive substances. If administrators at the University of Missouri had been correct that Mowrer's questionnaire actually harmed students, the university would have been justified in seeking to regulate it. The difficulty, of course, is that such matters are rarely clear-cut. Not only can the definition of "harm" be contentious, but frequently research creates merely the *risk* of harm, in which case it must be determined how to weigh such risk against potential gains to knowledge.

Such questions are the subject of a lively ongoing debate in the current controversy over the role of institutional review boards (IRBs).[27] IRBs are created by universities pursuant to federal mandate; they must review and approve certain research involving "human subjects." In today's university, Mowrer's questionnaire would probably have to be approved by an IRB, which would be empowered to compel Mowrer to redesign his study in a manner deemed adequate to protect the rights of his "human subjects." The appropriate balance between IRB regulation and academic freedom is widely contested in the academy.[28]

Freedom to Publish

Freedom of research cannot advance knowledge unless research results are circulated to the public for evaluation, assessment, and incorporation into ongoing debate. But public disclosure of research is often more embarrassing and controversial than the research itself. Recall how Cardinal Cajetan distinguished between freedom of intramural scholarly disputation and liberty to address the masses ("stupid people") whose faith might falter.

Scholarly publication can sometimes arouse and offend powerful constituencies—parents, alumni, and students —and embroil universities in controversies that threaten their financial resources. At a minimum, the unqualified affirmation of the 1940 *Statement* provides that when publication involves research conducted with professional standards of care, these consequences, however unnerving to university administrators and trustees, cannot justify censorship of publication.

A powerful and still-enduring statement on freedom of publication came not from Committee A directly but from a faculty committee at the University of Montana in 1918, which Committee A published in full when it closed the successfully resolved case. Louis Levine was an assistant professor of economics who, with the express encouragement of both the president and the chancellor of the university, undertook research on the subject of taxation in Montana. The first monograph he prepared was on the taxation of the mining industry, a controversial political issue at the time. After reading the manuscript and consulting with the governor of the state, the chancellor forbade Professor Levine to publish the work, in part because of what the chancellor saw as "personal bias" in Levine's analyses, but in much larger part so that the university would not be associated with the dispute. Professor Levine found an alternative venue in which to publish his monograph and was promptly suspended for his effort.

The university had recently revised its rules to create a committee composed of three faculty members—one appointed by the chancellor, one appointed by the president, and one elected by the faculty—to hear matters of suspension. Professor Levine appealed to that committee, which, surprisingly, unanimously found that Professor Levine had the right to ignore the chancellor's order and to publish his work; it rejected the charge of "insubordination" brought against him. The university's governing board then voted to sustain the suspension but to reinstate Professor Levine with full salary for its period. This Solomonic disposition closed the case, and Committee A, which had sent a representative to mediate the dispute, published an ample account that included the university committee's findings. The university committee's conclusions turned squarely on the difference between faculty as employees and faculty as appointees charged with the performance of a public function.

The committee is . . . of the opinion that the order of the Chancellor represents an unsound educational policy. In issuing this order the Chancellor assumed to direct the pronouncement of expert ·opinion by members of the faculty. . . .

If this policy [the Chancellor's] is carried out, it means that no member of the faculty may discuss any of the public questions under consideration at the present time, such as the tariff, the League of Nations, the control and ownership of railroads, health inspection in the schools, social control, political organizations, and the like. If professors of economics and politics can discuss none of these questions, their departments should not be permitted to continue in the University, for the very fact that we have men employed in these subjects implies that they must make a study of them and give the result of their investigations to the people of the state. It does not follow that their conclusions must be accepted, for the opinions of members of the faculty are worthy of consideration only so far as they are supported by indisputable facts and sound logic. In case their arguments are weak, the weakness can be detected and exposed. Nothing has been more the subject of party political differences than the tariff, and yet dozens of books on that subject have been written by university professors of economics in all parts of the country. They have written upon this subject, and their right to do so has never been denied, for the reason that it is one of the subjects they are employed to investigate and to teach in the class-room. A policy which forbids them to write upon that subject, or upon the subject of taxation, on the ground of non-interference in partisan politics, would equally require the elimination of such subjects from the university curriculum. . . .

Concerning the question of the policy above stated, some hold the opinion that as a railroad president may pigeon-hole the report of an engineer who has been sent out to investigate a building plan which an employed architect may have prepared with infinite pains, or as a capitalist may keep in his desk a report of any employee who has investigated a proposed project, so may the Chancellor withhold temporarily or permanently any report which may be prepared by faculty members, and which he may think should not be divulged.

The situations are not analogous. There is a vast different between a private trust and a public trust. The University belongs in the service of the people of the state. The Chancellor should not even claim the right or privilege of representing the people of the state. He should not say what the people shall or shall not hear or be told. If he is to be judge of what one may not say he must of necessity be judge of what one may say. He becomes the sole individual to decide, and on his decision will depend the policy of what the public shall or shall not be told by men who have devoted their lives to the study of particular subjects.[29]

Although the 1940 *Statement* speaks about the freedom to publish the results of "research," in modern times the question has arisen whether there ought also to be freedom to publish the results of artistic production. The public display of visual art, theater, or cinema is capable of sparking the most intense outrage.[30] Yet assimilating artistic expression to more traditional academic work is awkward, for it is not clear that artistic expression advances knowledge in the same way as traditional disciplinary scholarship.

When faced with this question, Committee A has tended to blur the distinction between freedom of publication of research and freedom of extramural speech. Freedom of extramural speech refers to the privilege of faculty to speak out about public matters unrelated to the narrow subject of their professional scholarship. A professor of law who publishes a salacious novel would be conceptualized as having engaged in a form of extramural speech. But a professor of English who publishes a novel could be conceptualized as publishing the analogy of "research" in her discipline. In the 1930s, Committee A investigated the refusal of Washington State College to reappoint a young assistant professor of English because his novel, *Angels on the Bough,* was said to disturb the college dean. Noting the "restrictive effect" that the college's action would likely "have upon creative writing," Committee A concluded that "it seems a sound proposition that a teacher who is a creative writer should have complete freedom of expression so long as his output does not conflict with the postal regulations or with other laws. He should not be made to suffer in his academic connection because what he writes is distasteful to an administrative officer. Any other rule would tend to make barren the college and university departments of English."[31]

Although Committee A referred to the case as evidencing an "improper restriction of literary freedom,"[32] it never explained whether artistic publication was analogous to freedom of research or to freedom of extramural speech. Committee A found itself in similarly murky straits when in 1960 yet another professor of English, this time at a religiously affiliated college, was discharged upon the publication of his novel *Brood of Fury*. Members of a local Catholic women's book club had termed the novel "the filthiest book they had ever read." The AAUP investigating committee issued a ringing but ambiguous affirmation of academic freedom. "As a member of the academic community of higher education in the United States and therefore sharing the goals, traditions, ideals, and spirit of that community, it is the duty of a college or university to withstand and to defend itself against 'censure' by its 'constituency' when the cause of the criticism is the responsible exercise of academic freedom by members of its faculty."[33]

The question of artistic speech was directly addressed in a statement titled *Academic Freedom and Artistic Expres-*

sion, issued hastily at the conclusion of a 1990 conference at Wolf Trap National Park for the Performing Arts. The statement was written by the AAUP, the American Council on Education, the Association of Governing Boards of Universities and Colleges, and the Wolf Trap Foundation for the Performing Arts. It is quite forceful, but not without conceptual difficulty.

> Faculty members and students engaged in the creation and presentation of works of the visual and the performing arts are as much engaged in pursuing the mission of the college or university as are those who write, teach, and study in other academic disciplines. Works of the visual and the performing arts are important both in their own right and because they can enhance our understanding of social institutions and the human condition. Artistic expression in the classroom, the studio, and the workshop therefore merits the same assurance of academic freedom that is accorded to other scholarly and teaching activities. Since faculty and student artistic presentations to the public are integral to their teaching, learning, and scholarship, these presentations merit no less protection. Educational and artistic criteria should be used by all who participate in the selection and presentation of artistic works.[34]

If Committee A situated freedom of artistic publication somewhere between freedom of research and freedom of extramural speech, the Wolf Trap statement situates freedom of artistic publication uncertainly between freedom of research and freedom of teaching. It imagines that the educational "mission" of a college or university includes instruction in the visual or performing arts and that this instruction intrinsically involves public presentations. It thus concludes that there must be freedom to publish the results reached "in the classroom, the studio, and the workshop." The same "educational and artistic criteria" that should govern classroom instruction should also govern "the selection and presentation of artistic works." This much is accordingly beyond dispute: *curricular* choice, including the choice to perform or display as an aspect of a school's or a department's instructional mission, is encompassed within the concept of freedom of teaching.[35]

Yet the Wolf Trap statement cannot quite bring itself to relinquish the additional argument that "the visual and the performing arts" produce knowledge by enhancing "our understanding of social institutions and the human condition." This argument would suggest that freedom of artistic publication should be conceptualized as a kind of freedom of research. The Wolf Trap statement does not earn this conclusion, however, for it fails to analyze whether the visual and performing arts produce the same kind of knowledge as "other scholarly . . . activities" and hence should merit analogous protection under freedom of research.

This perennial question of characterization is difficult. It turns on whether art produces forms of knowledge that can be advanced through the disciplinary methods characteristic of scholarship, or whether it instead creates forms of pleasure and insight that are particular and idiosyncratic. On the former supposition, art would merit the discrete and specialized protections of academic freedom of research, which is designed to promote knowledge through the exercise of distinctively professional norms. On the latter supposition, by contrast, art would receive only the protections that attach to the individual right of freedom of expression that is the entitlement of every person in a democracy. Artistic expression would constitute extramural expression, rather than research. We discuss the nature and scope of academic freedom of extramural expression in chapter 6. The production and display of works of art present aspects of academic freedom that have not yet been fully or adequately theorized.

CHAPTER 4

Freedom of Teaching

Academic freedom in the classroom is not a simple subject. The freedom of the individual professor in the classroom—what the Germans would call *Lehrfreiheit*—must be reconciled with the prerogative of the corporate body of the faculty to design and implement curricular requirements. There is also the question of *student* academic freedom, which the Germans would call *Lernfreiheit*.[1] *Lernfreiheit* never did make the transition to America, and in this country it is not clear whether it possesses independent content apart from the requirement that faculty abide by the proper limits of *Lehrfreiheit*.[2] It is in any event to the theoretical and practical substance of the latter that we turn in this chapter.

Theoretical Foundations

Important aspects of freedom of teaching derive directly from freedom of research and publication. Insofar as scholars are free to disseminate the results of their research to the general public and to disciplinary peers, they must also be free to disseminate these results to their students.[3] Freedom of teaching is in this sense an outgrowth of freedom of research and publication. But because faculty without research obligations can also claim academic freedom in the classroom, freedom of teaching is conceptually distinct from, and extends beyond, freedom of research and publication. Lecturers who are neither obligated nor expected to conduct research nevertheless enjoy academic freedom regarding their pedagogical responsibilities.

It might be thought that this aspect of academic freedom can be justified on the ground of professional expertise. University faculty are expert both in their scholarly discipline and in their pedagogical technique, so it can be argued that lay persons lack competence to control or evaluate methods of teaching. But this argument proves too much. It suggests that all expert professional teachers, from the kindergarten level up, should enjoy academic freedom in the classroom, and that is certainly not the case.[4]

Although the 1915 *Declaration* does not discount the role of disciplinary expertise, it ultimately asserts a different rationale for freedom of teaching. The *Declaration* begins with the premise that the purpose of university education is "not to provide . . . students with ready-made conclusions, but to train them to think for themselves, and to provide them access to those materials which they need if they are to think intelligently."[5] The *Declaration* then argues: "No man can be a successful teacher unless he enjoys the respect of his students, and their confidence in his intellectual integrity. It is clear, however, that this confidence will be impaired if there is suspicion on the part of the student that the teacher is not expressing himself fully or frankly. . . . It is not only the character of the instruction but also the character of the instructor that counts; and if the student has reason to believe that the instructor is not true to himself, the virtue of the instruction as an educative force is incalculably diminished."

The *Declaration* thus propounds an explicit theory of higher education. It proposes that the pedagogical purpose of universities and colleges is to instill in students the mature independence of mind that characterizes successful adulthood. Universities and colleges cannot fulfill this mission merely by conveying information or transmitting commonly accepted truths. Independence of mind is an active virtue, not a passive one. It cannot be drilled into students; it must be drawn out of them. It is a virtue that is acquired primarily through emulation. The essentially American premise of the *Declaration* is that students cannot learn how to exercise a mature independence of mind unless their instructors are themselves free to model independent thought in the classroom. This point had already been stressed by Josiah Royce two decades before the 1915 *Declaration:*

Advanced instruction aims to teach the opinions of an honest and competent man upon more or less doubtful question. . . . The advanced instructor . . . has to be responsible not only for his manner of presenting his doctrines, but for the doctrines themselves, which are not admitted dogmas, but ought to be his personal opinions. But responsibility and freedom are correlatives. If you force me to teach such and such dogmas, then you must be responsible for them, not I. I am your mouthpiece. But if I am to be responsible for what I say, then I must be free to say just what I think best. . . .

If such is the business of the teacher, viz., not merely to state his opinions, but to treat his pupils as embryo investigators, to be made into mature investigators as far as is possible, then surely the teacher must show himself as already an investigator. He need not be a great discoverer. Investigation is not usually discovery. . . . But to teach activity, the teacher must show activity. And of what use is the show unless the activity is certainly free?[6]

Different professors instill a mature independence of mind in different ways. Some refrain from articulating their own opinions; others set forth their own views but welcome critical discussion; still others exemplify the process of Socratic inquiry. It all depends on what the 1915 *Declaration* calls the "character of the instructor." It is difficult if not dangerous to attempt to lay down bright and abstract rules because the quality of the connection that professors forge with their students depends so heavily on individual style and personality.

The essential point is that a professor's pedagogical approach must educate students rather than indoctrinate them. The line between education and indoctrination cannot be drawn without reference to applicable professional norms. Consider, for example, a mathematics student who refuses to internalize and apply the proper rules for solving differential equations. If we conclude, as we are likely to do, that such a student is not exercising a mature independence of mind, but is instead displaying a stubborn refusal to learn, it is because the profession understands these aspects of mathematics to be dogmatic in character. We would apply the same analysis to the case of a medical student who refuses to accept the anatomical information provided by the instructor.

These examples illustrate that not every instructor who requires students mechanically to internalize and reproduce information, methodologies, or theories is guilty of indoctrination. But these examples should be contrasted with the case of an English student who refuses to agree with a professor's interpretation of *Paradise Lost.* Whether such a student is thinking for herself or instead stubbornly refusing to learn depends on our appraisal of the quality of the student's own countervailing interpretation of *Paradise Lost.* If an English instructor penalized a student simply for disagreeing, we would properly condemn the instructor for indoctrination. The very pedagogy that in a course on mathematics would constitute education might constitute indoctrination if pursued in an English course, and the difference would turn chiefly on the distinction between the way that the scholarly profession regards knowledge in mathematics and the way that it regards knowledge in English.

This suggests the accuracy of John Dewey's observation that indoctrination consists in dogmatically promulgating "*as truth* ideas or opinions"[7] that a discipline does not regard as dogmatically true. Scholars regard the truths of mathematics (or anatomy) as dogmatic in nature; they do not so regard the truths of literary criticism. As a consequence, pedagogical dynamics in classrooms devoted to mathematics differ from those in classrooms devoted to English.

This suggests that the distinction between indoctrination and education depends on relevant scholarly standards of knowledge. The point can be illustrated by the case of Allen Krebs, a sociologist who was in only his second year of teaching at Adelphi University when he was suspended in 1965.[8] Krebs was an avowed Marxist, whose views were well known to his department and to the administration when he was hired. What triggered his suspension and eventual non-reappointment was the midterm examination that he assigned to all three of his undergraduate classes—two introductory courses in sociology and an advanced course in the history of sociological thought in the nineteenth century. The examination consisted of thirty multiple-choice questions, including the following:

The clergy in the middle ages can be likened to:
(1) the army of today
(2) the propagandists of today
(3) the secret police of today
(4) all of the above
(5) none of the above.

The U.S. opposes the development of socialist societies because:
(1) socialism destroys people's freedom
(2) socialism provides an alternative to capitalist organization of society
(3) whenever socialism has appeared it has caused Americans to suffer
(4) socialism aims at the destruction of the U.S.
(5) all of the above.

A socialist perspective has made little headway in the U.S. because of:
(1) its vagueness and inaccuracy
(2) material circumstances are not yet present
(3) Americans cherish freedom too dearly
(4) socialism has everywhere created more suffering than it has cured
(5) socialism has no better answers than capitalism.

The AAUP committee investigating Krebs's suspension properly concluded that the midterm examination was "thoroughly unprofessional—badly drafted, ambiguous, tendentious, and prejudicial."[9] The examination exemplifies indoctrination because it attempts to extract from students dogmatic answers in matters about which the profession of sociology does not recognize dogmatic knowledge.[10] It would be an exercise of academic freedom for a professor to ask students in an economics examination to "compare and contrast" Karl Marx with Milton Friedman or even to ask students to explain whom they find more persuasive. It would also be an exercise of academic freedom to evaluate students on the quality of their responses, on their demonstrated mastery of Marx and Friedman. But it is indoctrination, rather than education, for an instructor to ask dogmatic questions that impose a "*truth*" of a matter as to which there is dispute within the discipline of economics. Dogmatic knowledge plays a different role in the discipline of mathematics than it does in the discipline of economics.[11]

Contemporary Controversies and Committee A Precedents

In recent years, classroom teaching in colleges and universities has been the subject of fierce political controversy. Professors are said to have so abused their academic freedom that legal intervention is necessary to protect students. These abuses are alleged to arise in at least three distinct ways. Professors are accused of intruding extraneous controversial matter, especially tendentious political or ideological commentary, into their teaching. They are charged with teaching without due regard for the exposition of contrary views and hence with failing to maintain the requisite "balance" and neutrality. They are condemned for teaching in ways that deeply offend the religious and political sensibilities of their students and hence for transforming their classrooms into hostile learning environments. In the remainder of this chapter we use applicable principles of academic freedom and relevant Committee A precedents to evaluate these charges.

The Injection of Irrelevant Controversy

The 1940 *Statement* provides that "teachers are entitled to freedom in the classroom in discussing their subject, but they should be careful not to introduce into their teaching controversial matter which has no relation to their subject." The *Statement* does not prohibit "controversial matter," only "controversial matter which has no relation" to the subject matter of a course.

In 1937 Edward Thorndike offered a classic exposition of the meaning of "controversial matter":

> A controversial subject oftenest means one where the opinions of fairly competent persons differ and are held with some pertinacity and vehemence. It is used especially where the division of opinion relates to matters of acknowledged public concern, such as, in the past, Protestantism, witchcraft, the divine right of kings, slavery, property requirements for suffrage, or free schools. Among such, now, are tariffs, government ownership of public utilities, international court, the New Deal, divorce, sterilization of idiots, insane, and criminals of certain sorts. . . . More broadly, a controversial subject is any that causes conflict or dispute, even though all the really competent persons are on one side, even though the conflict is waged with restraint and urbanity, even though the subject is caviar to the general.[12]

In 1970, the joint drafting organizations appended an interpretive comment to the 1940 *Statement* that stressed the importance of controversy within higher education: "The intent of this statement is not to discourage what is 'controversial.' Controversy is at the heart of the free academic inquiry which the entire statement is designed to foster. The passage serves to underscore the need for teachers to avoid persistently intruding material which has no relation to their subject."

Although recently proposed state legislation provides that students enrolled in institutions of higher education have a right not to have their "academic freedom" infringed "by instructors who persistently introduce controversial matter into the classroom,"[13] the profession has consistently upheld an instructor's right to teach using controversial material so long as it is pedagogically relevant. Consider, for example, the case of Professor Robert F. McClellan, whose probationary appointment in the department of history was not renewed in 1967 by Edgar L. Harden, the president of Northern Michigan University.[14] President Harden's decision was based in part on the allegation that McClellan had "misused" the classroom. McClellan was an activist who had supported the efforts of local community groups to block the university's planned expansion into their neighborhood. McClellan had assigned students to interview residents about their views on the university's expansion plan. The faculty senate at Northern Michigan considered President Harden's allegation and vindicated Professor McClellan, noting that the assignment had been organized by McClellan's class itself as a result of a classroom discussion about possible tensions between private and public interests. The AAUP investigating committee concurred in the faculty's judgment.

Also relevant is the case of H. Brent Davis, a beginning instructor in speech at Arkansas Agricultural and Mechanical College, who was summarily dismissed in 1965 by the institution's board of trustees. Davis was teaching Speech 273, a course in "argumentation and debate." He had become personally involved in a very public debate in Arkansas over the use of corporal punishment in prisons, and he had assigned "anti-strap" petitions in his class for students either to affirm or to denounce as part of an exercise in opinion formation and expression.[15] Davis told a reporter covering the controversy that the assignment was "an 'academic exercise' for an Argumentation and Debate class which he teaches at A. & M. He said the petitions were not being circulated for political purposes, even though he personally believes the strap shouldn't be used on prisoners. 'This is not a drive,' he said. 'Nothing will be done with the petitions. I certainly wouldn't do anything with them without clearing it with my superiors. That's a matter of professional ethics.'" "Apparently," the investigating committee observed, "a number of students did not distinguish between the petition as a device to investigate the students' willingness to form opinions and the petition as propaganda against corporal punishment of convicts." The dean of academic affairs defended Davis's use of the petition for the former purpose as "in the best tradition" of teaching rational argument. The investigating committee concluded that the dismissal violated the 1940 *Statement*.[16]

Both McClellan and Davis brought highly political controversies directly into their classrooms. Their assignments were especially inflammatory because of their own obvious political commitments. Yet in each case the assignment was plainly material to the subject matter of the class, and, nota bene, there was no evidence of indoctrination, no sign that either McClellan or Davis had required students to accept his own political position. However controversial their teaching assignments, they were protected by "freedom in the classroom" under the 1940 *Statement.*

It goes without saying that valuable class time should not be squandered on educationally irrelevant frolics. A student of classical history has every right to complain if class time is consumed by an instructor's tirades on intramural disputes in the History Department; a student of American letters has every right to complain if class time is devoted to an instructor's monologues on his or her personal life; and so on. The McClellan and Davis cases thus require us to take literally the words of 1940 *Statement:* if controversial material is to be excluded from the classroom, it is because such material "has no relation" to the pedagogical subject at issue in the classroom.

Recent charges of classroom abuse have thus tended to stress that professors inject controversial material into their classrooms without pedagogical justification. Consider, for example, the advice that Students for Academic Freedom (SAF) distributes to its members: "If you are not taking a course whose subject is the war in Iraq, your professor should not be making statements about the war in class. Or about George Bush, if the class is not on contemporary American presidents, presidential administrations or some similar subject."[17] This and similar complaints require us to clarify the criteria of pedagogical relevance.

This issue is not new. It arose early in the last century when the *New Republic* published a scathing critique of the language in the 1925 conference statement (see chapter 2) prohibiting instructors from introducing into their classrooms "controversial and irrelevant subjects outside" their own "field of study."[18]

The terms of this bargain are perfectly clear: the professor is absolutely free to do what he is employed to do. Let us suppose that he is engaged to teach French. So long as he rehearses his students in irregular conjugations, devoting his leisure hours to papers on the place of Rousseau in the Romantic Movement, his freedom is to be treasured like a fine pearl of great price. But if he says to his innocents that Rousseau was a single-taxer, he may be called up to the presidential sanctum for a wigging. Taxation may be mentioned only by the professor duly licensed to mention it. . . .

[The professor's "own field of study"] is a convenient phrase which anyone might use to indicate the point of departure of his thoughts, without in the least intending to exclude himself from whatever other fields might tempt his roving eye. According to such a latitudinarian definition we might consider every man's field to be the universe as viewed from the point of vantage of his specialized technique. If that technique is the French language, then he may of course discuss any ideas that can be discussed in French, or any subjects to which he is led by reading French. But is this the meaning the conventions on academic freedom intend? Certainly not. What is the sense of saying that no teacher may discuss "controversial topics outside his own field" if you mean that his field is whatever he is led to discuss? These rules are intended to mean something, and what this one is intended to mean turns upon a rigorously narrow conception of the professors' field. It means that the professor who is hired to parse French sentences must to stick to parsing. There the "university or college may not impose any limitation upon the teacher's freedom."[19]

It is no doubt in response to this and like criticism that the 1940 *Statement* quite deliberately contains no equivalent language limiting pedagogy to a professor's "field of study."[20] Instead the 1940 *Statement* accords professors "freedom in the classroom in discussing their subject," provided that they do not "introduce into their teaching controversial matter which has no relation to their subject." The question is therefore what it means for teaching material to bear a "relation" to a subject under pedagogical consideration.

We propose the following criterion: A pedagogical intervention bears a "relation" to a subject under consideration if it is educationally relevant. A pedagogical intervention is educationally relevant if it assists students in better understanding a subject under consideration, either in the sense of acquiring greater cognitive mastery of that subject or in the sense of acquiring a more mature apprehension of the import of that subject, which is to say, an improved ability to experience and appreciate the significance of that subject.

On the cognitive side, the trend toward interdisciplinarity demonstrates how difficult it is to divide knowledge into hermetically disconnected domains. Conrad Russell, discussing the question of curricular authority, has pointed out "that all knowledge can be related to all other knowledge (given enough ingenuity) and what background knowledge any teacher finds necessary to the understanding of his subject may depend on his approach to that subject." Russell notes that students should be welcome to apply what they have learned in one class to the subject matter of another, even to the extent of challenging an instructor by "drawing background from a field with which [the instructor] is unfamiliar."[21] (Recall that such challenges were exactly those posed by Christian Wolff's students to the discomfiture of the theologians at the University of Halle in the 1720s.) The standard is whether material from a seemingly foreign field of study illuminates the subject matter under scrutiny, bearing in mind that the overall design of a modern curriculum is to provide a general education, which is to say, the ability to think systemically and in an independent and informed manner.

On the heuristic side, the pedagogical question that all instructors face is how to encourage students to care enough about the subject matter of a course to engage actively with its significance. Students cannot acquire habits of independent thought unless they learn to grapple hard and seriously with curricular material. They must be motivated to do so.[22] Their attention must be enlivened so that they can fully appreciate the normative stakes in forming one or another assessment of a subject under consideration. How instructors seek to elicit this response from students is highly personal and contextual because it depends heavily on a chemistry of personality that differs from professor to professor, and indeed from classroom to classroom.

The advice of SAF should be evaluated from this perspective. The organization assumes that if the "subject" of a course is not "the war in Iraq," professors ought not to "be making statements about the war in class." It assumes that if a course "is not on contemporary American presidents," professors ought not to be making statements about George Bush. But SAF implicitly defines educational relevance in terms of the description of a course catalog. It misses entirely the heuristic necessity of actively arousing student attention and interest. So long as indoctrination is not at issue, there is nothing wrong with an instructor in ancient history drawing a parallel between Roman domination of Palestine and the present war in Iraq, if by so doing he or she can enliven student discussion and debate.[23] The comparison is educationally relevant if it serves proper pedagogical purposes. A similar analysis would apply to an instructor in English history who seeks to interest students by suggesting parallels between King George III's conduct of the Revolutionary War and President Bush's conduct of the war in Iraq.[24] The scope of educational relevance is to be determined not by the contents of a course catalog but by the heuristic purposes and consequences of a pedagogical intervention.

This has long been the judgment of Committee A. Consider, for example, the dismissal in 1934 of associate professor of history Ralph E. Turner by the University of Pittsburgh, in part because he sought to make history come

alive for the students in his survey course. As the AAUP
investigating committee explained:

> Dr. Turner believes in the cultural interpretation of history.
> Such an interpretation has, as a concomitant, implications
> likely to prove uncomfortable to some. Dr. Turner is a realist
> and one who looks at the facts of history realistically. He
> sought to make students understand that the historical per-
> sons of the past were real persons, possessing both virtues
> and vices and that they have their counterpart in others to-
> day. His choice of historical and present-day evidence and
> illustrations used in this comparative process was doubt-
> less not always wise and caused some misunderstanding
> and criticism. In studying social conflicts and social traits
> he urged the students to observe those about them today,
> stressing the fact that the ever-shifting social processes are
> the stuff of history.
>
> Dr. Turner taught the Survey Course frankly from the
> viewpoint of common men and their status under different
> economic, social, and political conditions. Because of this
> fact he was regarded by some, including the Chancellor, as
> a propagandist. Also at times he jumped the gap between
> the past and the present in order to compare and contrast
> the past with the present. This procedure the Committee be-
> lieves was not for the purpose of commenting on present-
> day conditions, as some criticism of his work implies, but
> rather to create in the minds of the students a consciousness
> of historical continuity and development.[25]

Turner was dismissed in part because some students were
offended by his attempts to instill an appreciation of the

significance of history by invoking recent events and contemporary personages. There is no doubt that Committee A
considered this aspiration to be an appropriate—if not admirable—pedagogical goal, even if it tended to make some
students more sympathetic to Turner's point of view.[26]

Committee A has consistently maintained this position.
In 1940, it considered the dismissal of Philip Mankin, who
had taught English for fourteen years at the State Teachers
College at Murfreesboro, Tennessee. Mr. Mankin's pastor
described him as a "Christian liberal" housed in what
Committee A's report found to be a religiously conservative albeit public institution of higher education. Mankin's
dismissal was based in part on the charge that he had introduced "controversial religious questions into classroom
discussion." The only specific example given the investigating committee was that during a class lecture on Greek
literature—and with reference to a specific passage in the
text under discussion—Mr. Mankin said that "he personally did not believe in a 'burning hell.'" The report noted
Mr. Mankin's explanation: "When religious subjects were
relevant to topics under discussion in the classroom, Mr.
Mankin believed that, rather than to avoid subjects of controversy, it was good teaching to permit their introduction
because of the stimulation of the thought of students
which would be the consequence of their careful and
impartial discussion." The investigating committee stated
that the "evidence shows that Mr. Mankin accepted only
those opportunities to discuss religious subjects that arose
naturally, and did not seek to create such opportunities or
to permit classroom discussions that were irrelevant, ir-

reverent, partisan, or unsympathetic." The committee concluded that Mankin's dismissal violated the 1940 *Statement.*[27]

Consider also the dismissal in 1948 of George F. Parker, an assistant professor of religion and philosophy at Evansville College. Parker was accused of introducing "political discussion" into his classes. The allegation was made on the basis of the statements of seven students, which the AAUP investigating committee summarized as follows: "Professor Parker encouraged a considerable amount of student discussion in the classroom, some of it only remotely connected with his courses. In illustration of logical propositions, fallacies, etc., he often chose material which reflected his own special viewpoints. His sympathy with the Wallace movement was obvious. He was critical of certain governmental policies, both national and local. His comments ranged widely, and included such varied topics as *Time,* the newspapers' handling of Wallace news, local civic conditions, military men, the police, and the merits of *Gentleman's Agreement.* His language was sometimes too caustic, and sometimes included derogatory epithets, one of which was applied to the President of the United States [Harry S. Truman]."

Professor Parker said this of his student critics: "I don't think my former mention of Wallace was irrelevant to the subject-matter of the course. Must I teach the logic of statistics and keep the whole discussion socially inconsequential, for fear of treading on dangerous ground? How could I teach Amos, Isaiah, Jesus, Kant, or John Dewey without running the risk of making some statement which might be called partisan? Is it education if you just transfer subject-matter without trying to elicit new evaluations?"

The AAUP investigating committee found no support for the conclusion that Professor Parker had used the classroom for overt propagandistic purposes, despite the fact that he did infuse his teaching with his political perspective. To the investigating committee, the dividing line between the relevant and irrelevant invocation of a political perspective turned on pedagogical purpose and effect, on the manner and spirit of a professor's classroom speech:

> Aside from uncertainties as to what is "controversial" and what is "related," all experienced teachers realize that it is neither possible nor desirable to exclude rigidly all controversial subjects, or all topics upon which the teacher is not an expert. Many things introduced into the classroom—illustrative material or applications, overtones of significance, illuminating *obiter dicta*—may not be in the bond as far as the subject of the course is concerned, but these and kindred techniques may be of the essence of good teaching. Such techniques are readily distinguishable from calculated, overt "propaganda." . . .

> In the nature of the case, judgments concerning the handling of controversial material will frequently depend not so much on the *what* as the *how*. As the late Charles A. Beard put it: "The exercise of a right is always a matter of method, means, spirit, and emphasis . . . Almost anything can be said on any subject on any occasion if the appropriate language is chosen." The total effect of what a teacher says on controversial subjects in the classroom depends a great deal upon the manner, the spirit in which he says it, and the emphasis he places upon it. It depends also upon

the previous existence of a relationship of confidence and understanding between the teacher and his students.[28]

Such judgments, the committee concluded, are necessarily contextual. They cannot be governed by mechanical and inflexible rules of the kind advanced by SAF.

That is not to say that anything goes in a classroom, as Committee A's case law evidences. On April 5, 1968, the day after Dr. Martin Luther King Jr. was assassinated, David E. Green, a first-year assistant professor of history at the Ohio State University, entered his eleven o'clock class entitled American Foreign Policy to 1914 and proclaimed that in light of the tragic events of the preceding day he had something more important to discuss than Jay's Treaty. Responding to a student question, Green announced that he had "suspended the curriculum," and he then spoke for the next forty-five minutes on Dr. King's assassination. Afterward, he burned his draft card as an expression of his opposition to all violence.[29]

The administration brought charges contemplating Green's dismissal before a faculty hearing committee. The committee found grounds to criticize severely the instructor's conduct, but determined that dismissal was not warranted. The board of trustees dismissed Green nonetheless. The AAUP investigating committee concurred with the faculty hearing committee that Professor Green had engaged in an act of symbolic political protest and in so doing had wrongly used his instructional role. Green's announcement that he had "suspended the curriculum" was inadequate to alert students that class had been canceled and that, by remaining, they would be subjected to a political speech. Howsoever heartfelt, howsoever deeply held, Green's oration was an avowedly political act, and academic freedom afforded David Green no right to commandeer the class for a "teach-in" on his personal political views.[30]

Balance

Modern critics of the academy frequently call for "more balanced, genuinely tolerant teaching on the part of faculties."[31] This call is usually justified by the observation that there is a "marked political imbalance among college faculty"[32] because the professoriat is said to be heavily slanted toward the political left. Whatever the truth of the latter assertion,[33] it is in the most fundamental sense irrelevant because academic freedom demands that faculty be judged on the professional merit of their work and not on their political affiliation or outlook. For purposes of institutional decision making, the political affiliation or religious belief of faculty simply ought not to matter.[34]

What ought to matter, as David Hollinger reminds us, is "first, the fidelity of the department to the broad contours of the learned discipline it is charged with representing on a given campus and second, the assurance that those contours are determined by the distinctive aims and methods of the relevant scientific and scholarly communities." "*To be balanced,*" Hollinger continues, "*is simply to do an academic project professionally. To be imbalanced is to leave out of account something that the academic norms of evidence and reasoning in the interest of truth require you to take into account.*"[35]

Hollinger's point is that the concept of balance makes sense in the context of academic freedom only by reference to the professional norms of a relevant scholarly community. There are scholarly disciplines in which certain models, theories, or concepts are so inextricably connected to a subject that to ignore or even to slight them is a dereliction of professional duty. One cannot teach biology without taking up evolution;[36] one cannot teach physical geology without dealing with plate tectonics; one cannot teach particle physics without engaging quantum electrodynamics. To teach such subjects is to assume the responsibility of covering material that is understood by scholars in the field as essential to its comprehension. Thus even a biologist who personally rejects the theory of evolution could not competently teach a course in population dynamics that fails to explicate evolutionary theory. In this narrow sense, "balance" may be required by the professional standards of particular disciplines.[37]

It is plain, however, that those who demand a "more balanced" pedagogy do not have this narrow concept of balance in mind. Their charges of "faculty imbalance" are rarely justified by specific disciplinary standards. They instead press the abstract complaint that "professors should give a fair presentation to alternative points of view." They assert that "professors should not use the classroom for proselytizing," but "should present alternative points of view fairly" and "should assign readings representing multiple views."[38]

To assess the significance of this general line of argument, we must ask how "alternative points of view" should be identified and "fairness" measured. It helps to consider the argument concretely. Consider how this standard might be applied to a course on the moral philosophy of Immanuel Kant. It would not be professionally incompetent for an instructor in a class on Kant to fail to expose students to the "alternative" views of Jeremy Bentham; nor would it be unfair if such an instructor failed to explain to students the competing views of David Hume. In a discipline like philosophy there are often innumerable "alternative points of view" that can considered. There is no meaningful sense in which an instructor can be required to represent competing philosophers or theories "fairly." In such a context, the abstract call for "balance" is logically and educationally incoherent.

Those who criticize faculty for "imbalance" typically are not concerned with subjects that possess the intellectual structure of particle physics or biology, in which a narrow sense of "balance" flows from the intrinsic disciplinary standards that define a subject matter. Those complaining of imbalance tend instead to focus on "soft" disciplines like philosophy, English, sociology, or political theory. Their complaint almost always turns on the charge that pedagogy is *politically* imbalanced. They express the fear that "whole colleges and universities have become dominated by a political ideology" and "ignore scholarly views that lie contrary to that ideology."[39] They are mostly concerned with only one form of "balance," which is the political balance between left and right.

This concern is sometimes explicit, as when the Committee for a Better Carolina denounced *Nickel and Dimed* as "an all-out assault on Christians, conservatives and capitalism."[40] The "balance" sought by the committee had nothing to do with disciplinary standards and everything to do with forcing the University of North Carolina to assign material awarding equal time to the committee's own conservative views. The concern for political balance is sometimes implicit. The charge that professors are using classroom discussion and assignments "for proselytizing," for example, suggests the fear that professors are communicating one politically salient viewpoint without also communicating the opposite viewpoint. The silent assumption seems to be that the classroom ought to be a site of political neutrality. It is clear, however, that any requirement of political balance or political neutrality would be inconsistent with elementary principles of academic freedom.

A requirement of political balance or political neutrality would compel faculty to present all sides of politically controversial questions. Any such obligation would be flatly incompatible with a scholar's accountability to professional standards. Consider the case of a biologist who teaches the theory of evolution. The theory of evolution happens to be politically controversial because the literal truth of the Bible is today a matter of political debate. To require a biologist to give equal time to a theory of intelligent design, simply because lay persons who are politically mobilized believe this theory, is to say that a scholar must in the name of political balance present as credible ideas that the scholarly profession repudiates as false. The whole

point of academic freedom is to insulate professional judgment from this kind of crude political control. Academic
freedom obligates scholars to use disciplinary standards,
not political standards, to guide their teaching.

Because contemporary scholarship embraces all matters
of human concern, scholarly ideas can become politically
controversial in a virtually infinite variety of ways. A rule
of political neutrality would require faculty to remain constantly vigilant concerning the political salience of ideas
expressed in the classroom; it would require them to present "alternative points of view" "fairly" whenever an idea
expressed in the classroom is infused with a sufficient degree of political controversy.[41] It is easy to see how such a
rule would suppress classroom discussion and undermine
the heuristic goal of producing students able to exercise a
mature independence of mind. It is precisely because of
the importance of this heuristic goal that freedom of teaching mandates that faculty be free to structure and discuss
classroom material as they deem most pedagogically effective, so long as they do not indoctrinate their students or
violate professional standards of pedagogical relevance
and substantive competence.

Hostile Environment

Contemporary critics of higher education charge that faculty have created a hostile educational environment. In the
words of a proposed statute "concerning students' rights in
higher education" that was introduced in the Colorado legislature, "Students have a right to expect that their aca-

demic freedom will not be infringed by instructors who create a hostile environment toward their political or religious beliefs."[42]

The idea of a "hostile environment" derives from anti-discrimination law. Employers violate the civil rights of employees if they permit the workplace to become a hostile environment for women or minorities. Critics of higher education wish to appropriate this idea and apply it to the context of university teaching. As with the ideal of "balance," there is a sense in which the idea is appropriately deployed. Professional ethics require faculty to "demonstrate respect for students" and to avoid "any exploitation, harassment, or discriminatory treatment."[43] Freedom of teaching would thus not protect a professor from disciplinary action if he were to harass, ridicule, or discriminate against students for their political or religious beliefs.

It is important, however, to distinguish between respect for persons and respect for ideas. Faculty must respect students as persons, but they needn't respect ideas, even ideas held by students. In higher education no idea is immune from potentially scathing criticism. If a student identifies with his own ideas, he might well experience ruthless critique of these ideas as a personal assault. But it is precisely the pedagogical purpose of higher education to introduce critical distance between students and their own ideas.

This point is illustrated by the case of Professor Ralph Turner, which we discussed earlier in this chapter. The stated ground of Turner's dismissal was that his attitude toward religion was "flippant and sneering" and that he sought to break down the faith of his students. The AAUP investigating committee interviewed a number of students representing a broad distribution of interests and three major faiths.

> There was testimony which indicated that some of Dr. Turner's remarks were misconstrued by some students, and in some cases were communicated to parents out of their setting, and hence in a way to foster misinterpretation and misunderstanding.
>
> Some parents, it was evident, were considerably disturbed. Two or three of the students indicated that they themselves had been disturbed by some of Dr. Turner's remarks. They said that he had upset some of their previous beliefs, but as they had studied further, read more widely, and found that other professors in other courses were making similar statements, they now knew that certain details of their pre-college beliefs were not essential to their faith. Typical of this testimony was the statement of one student that she was greatly disturbed when, in the course of a class discussion, the statement was made that there were different versions of the Garden of Eden story.
>
> One student, however, said he thought Dr. Turner was a menace to the Christian faith, and should not be allowed to teach in a Christian school. He said that he thought the church should never be criticized.[44]

The student who proclaimed that "the church should never be criticized" is an example of someone so identified with his own beliefs as to be intolerant of their critical evaluation. This student experienced Turner as a "menace" and no doubt today would have charged Turner with creating a "hostile environment" for his religious views. If the prohibition of a "hostile environment" means that professors must not threaten students in the security of their "political or religious beliefs," it signifies that faculty are to be prevented from modeling the critical thought and inquiry that is the central pedagogical purpose of higher education. Because the charge of a "hostile environment" confuses respect for persons with respect for ideas, it is fundamentally inconsistent with freedom of teaching.

The idea of a "hostile environment" is relatively new, so there are no Committee A precedents that directly evaluate the idea. But the distinction between respect for persons and respect for ideas was a persistent theme of academic freedom throughout the twentieth century. Consider the 1967 dismissal of Scott Chisholm, an instructor at Indiana State University, for burning an American flag in his classroom. Chisholm's conduct might well have violated the proposed Colorado statute prohibiting the creation of a hostile environment for the "political beliefs" of students.

Mr. Chisholm had been teaching courses on writing for three years. He was a countercultural campus figure: students had complained of his reading e. e. cummings in an advanced class in creative writing; he had started a coffeehouse where poetry was read and over which the town police maintained closer than usual surveillance; and so on. What happened in his English composition class on April 12, 1967, was recounted by the AAUP investigating committee:

According to Mr. Chisholm, in testimony given later before a faculty hearing committee and not substantially disputed by testimony of students before the same committee, his objective on April 12 was to have the class recognize the difference between "concrete" and "abstract" aspects of language, and that (in his words) "the two essential qualities could be separated"—that, in other words, objects could be viewed as objects, without the involvement of their abstract (or symbolic) meaning. In this connection, he discussed a newspaper report from the *Christian Science Monitor* concerning the burning of an American flag by French leftists. He commented, according to his later testimony, that in such cases it is important to differentiate the symbolic implication of the act from the object which has been destroyed, and that people should be aware of possible entrapment by their own symbols. He recalled having then said, "Any man could burn any flag so long as it is understood that he is not attacking the abstract value for which the flag stands—that he is not entering into an unpatriotic act or a quarrel with his government or with its principles— that he is merely burning a concrete object." He added that he would be willing to burn any flag himself, to quote his subsequent words, "so long as the context in which I am burning it is understood—that I am burning it as a concrete object as opposed to a symbol of abstract values—that I am not burning it as an unpatriotic act."[45]

A student alerted her father, who in turn complained to Indiana State's president that an instructor said that he would burn an American flag. The president referred the matter to the vice president. On April 14, a student who was auditing the class placed a small American flag propped in a spool on the instructor's desk accompanied by a book of matches. She did this, she later testified, because "I wanted to show him up and to show that I loved my country." When Mr. Chisholm entered the classroom and saw the flag and matches on the desk,

he picked up the matches and burned the flag, announcing as he did so that he was not thereby attacking the government of the United States. He recalled having said: "This is not to be misconstrued as an unpatriotic act, because I am not here involved with abstract questions about the values of my government, about its foreign policy, or about its actions. I am not attacking the principles for which it stands, nor am I making a political comment about democracy. I am burning a concrete object—a stick and a piece of cloth—not my country or its principles." After putting the flag in a sink in the room, he continued to discuss the meaning of the act, using various analogies. There was no disturbance in the class and no special reaction.[46]

Dismissal proceedings were initiated on charges of "unprofessional conduct." After a full hearing, a faculty committee made four findings: (1) that Mr. Chisholm burned a small American flag in his English 102 class; (2) that the act was within the context and scope of English 102; (3) that Mr. Chisholm had evidenced no malice toward or disrespect for the United States by the act; and (4) that Mr. Chisholm's action "constituted 'unprofessional conduct' in that it demonstrated poor judgment, a failure to exercise proper restraint, and a failure to control the context in which his demonstration occurred—and thus brought embarrassment to the University."[47] The faculty hearing committee recommended that Mr. Chisholm be censured and that the board of trustees consider the renewal (or nonrenewal) of his appointment at the conclusion of its term. Instead, Chisholm was dismissed by the board.

The AAUP investigating committee faulted the faculty hearing committee as well as the administration and governing board. It reasoned that if the hearing committee's first three findings were supported by the evidence, as they were, Chisholm's punishment for burning the flag "denied the teacher freedom in the classroom to discuss his subject" as provided for in the 1940 *Statement.* The hearing committee had in its fourth finding essentially defined the boundaries of faculty professionalism in terms of "public indignation and pressure." Committee A affirmed that the propriety of teaching in higher education should instead be determined by the disciplinary standard of educational relevance.

Popular indignation can arise whenever faculty are perceived to disrespect cherished ideas and values. But if a major purpose of higher education is to instill independence of mind, faculty must be free to question received wisdom. It is inevitable that some students will experience such criticism as hostility and personal disrespect. That is why professional standards have always excluded public indignation as a justifiable ground for circumscribing academic freedom. Chisholm's toy-flag burning may well have created a "hostile environment" for the "political beliefs" of some of his students; it may well have been pedagogically unnecessary; and it may well have expressed an intellectual idea that was jejune. But Chisholm's action was pedagogically relevant and did not constitute indoctrination. It was therefore protected by academic freedom to teach.

The point has been well summarized by Mark Taylor, commenting on the challenge posed by today's "religiously correct" students: "For years, I have begun my classes by telling students that if they are not more confused and uncertain at the end of the course than they were at the beginning, I will have failed. A growing number of religiously correct students consider this challenge a direct assault on their faith. Yet the task of thinking and teaching, especially in an age of emergent fundamentalisms, is to cultivate a faith in doubt that calls into question every certainty."[48] All too often a "hostile educational environment" may merely be one in which faculty have not allowed students to rest complacently and comfortably with their beliefs.

To punish faculty for creating a hostile environment would, as a practical matter, put instructors at the mercy of students who are unable or unwilling to distance themselves critically from their own most cherished ideas and thus unable or unwilling to distinguish an educational exercise from a political statement. As Josiah Royce observed more than a century ago, such constraints would suppress education in the classroom, for no instructor could ever know "when he will be accused of atheism for having mentioned in his classroom Voltaire, without warning his pupils against Voltaire's books."[49]

CHAPTER 5

Freedom of Intramural Expression

Scholars of academic freedom distinguish between freedom of intramural expression and freedom of extramural expression. These categories turn not on the location of faculty speech but on its substance. "Intramural expression," the subject of this chapter, concerns faculty speech that does not involve disciplinary expertise but is instead about the action, policy, or personnel of a faculty member's home institution. Freedom of intramural expression encompasses both a letter in the local press protesting a university's decision to displace residents of adjoining low-income neighborhoods and a motion made to the same effect in a faculty senate or council. "Extramural expression," the subject of chapter 6, concerns faculty speech that involves neither disciplinary expertise nor the subject matter of a faculty member's home institution. Freedom of extramural expression instead applies to communications made by professors in their role as citizens of the larger body politic. A letter to a student newspaper protesting the war in Iraq would be considered an extramural expression, as would a similar letter to the *New York Times.*

Theoretical Foundations

When American academic reformers looked to the German university as a model, they encountered an institution that, although subservient to the state in terms of financing and even in matters of faculty selection, was in all other essentials self-governing. Faculty members were accorded a degree of independence unknown in American higher education of the period. German universities did not have presidents or administrative vice presidents or active governing boards. Rectors and deans were customarily selected from the faculty, and they returned to the faculty after their service. American faculties, by contrast, found themselves placed in institutions that were governed as if they were corporations. Such institutions sought to treat faculty as mere employees. That status, as we have seen, was in serious contradiction to basic guarantees of academic freedom.

Three potential strategies emerged to resolve this tension. The first and most radical was advocated by James McKeen Cattell of Columbia University, who demanded that faculty control institutions of higher education.[1] Cattell's demand was not attractive to the draftsmen of the

1915 *Declaration*, who were all major figures in their disciplines and not about to embark upon so quixotic a quest.

The second strategy was for faculty to accept the legal position of employees and attempt to preserve academic freedom of teaching and research within its confines. What that position implied was captured in C. B. Labatt's eight-volume treatise on the law of master and servant published in 1913. Professors, like all employees, would have to be "respectful and free from insolence"[2] toward their employers; they would have to obey all their employers' reasonable orders.[3] Professors would have to fulfill a "duty of loyalty" by refraining from acts likely to produce a detriment to their employers; they could not offend persons having dealings with their employers, act or even speak in ways likely to injure their employers' standing, or excite "discontent" among subordinates or coworkers.[4] The second strategy would have required faculty to accept this thick set of obligations in return for an institution's promise not to regulate research or teaching. "It is in this environment," Cattell remarked, that a professor might "sometimes enjoy[] the academic freedom which allows him to teach that two and two do make four in spite of any prejudice to the contrary in the community."[5]

The drafters of the 1915 *Declaration* charted a third course—more subtle than Cattell's but, in a sense, no less radical. The *Declaration* did not advocate any change in the legal position of faculty; in the eyes of the law, faculty would remain employees. The *Declaration* sought instead to change institutional practices by altering the perception of faculty *status*—a strategy that would today be termed "soft law" in contrast to Cattell's demand for a shift in the "hard law" of faculty legal control. The *Declaration* strove to make "still more clear the nature of the relationship between university trustees and members of university faculties. The latter are the appointees, but not in any proper sense the employees, of the former." The consequence of this altered status bulked large: "A university is a great and indispensable organ of the higher life of a civilized community, in the work of which the trustees hold an essential and highly honorable place, but in which the faculties hold an *independent* place, with quite *equal* responsibilities—and in relation to purely scientific and educational questions, the primary responsibility."[6]

The authors of the *Declaration* sought to have faculty regarded as "independent" and "equal" participants in the university. They refused to accept the position of mere hired hands. In the Progressive media of the time, "the very terms of mastery and service used to justify administrative control took on a pejorative meaning. . . . The professor was not to be made a 'hireling,' a 'servant,' a 'mere employee,' a 'hired-man,' a 'place-holder' (John Dewey's phrase), or, more colorfully, a 'subservient coward.'"[7] Implicit in the *Declaration*'s attempt to revise the status of faculty lay a theory of freedom of intramural speech and action. But this theory remained latent; the *Declaration* neither named nor discussed questions of intramural speech. These were to be worked out on a case-by-case basis throughout the remainder of the twentieth century.

Committee A Precedents before 1940

Several investigations before 1940 explored what it meant for faculty to hold an "equal" and "independent" place within the university. We discuss four in particular, because they well illustrate how the question developed in the years leading up to the 1940 *Statement.*

The AAUP's very first investigation was into the dismissal of Professor A. A. Knowlton at the University of Utah in 1915. It involved the question whether an employee's duty of respect to his employer applied to the professoriat. Professor Knowlton was overheard in private conversation to have said, "Isn't it too bad that we have a man like that as Chairman of the Board of Regents!"[8] He was consequently dismissed for "speaking very disrespectfully" of the chairman.[9] The board issued a public statement defending its action:

It is argued to the Board that professors and instructors should have the right of free thought, free speech and free action. This cannot be and is not questioned. The Board, however, has the same rights. These privileges are reciprocal. When the rights of the two clash, then it is for the Board to determine which is right and which course serves, or is inimical to, the best interests of the University. . . .

Dr. Knowlton . . . has seen fit to speak very disrespectfully, if not insultingly, of the Chairman of the Board of Regents. From his standpoint, this doubtless means that he has exercised his inalienable rights of free thought, free speech and free action. But the President and the Board also have an equal right to free thought, free speech and free action, with the result that the President and the Board do not agree with Dr. Knowlton's sentiments; he may hereafter find an institution and State where similar sentiments against the presiding officer of the governing board may be approved. If so, that is where he belongs.

The AAUP investigating committee dismissed the charge of disrespect outright: "The law of *lèse-majesté* cannot with advantage ... be applied to university faculties in America." It went on to address the regents' claim that the goal of "efficiency" justified the removal of any personnel who caused "friction" with the university administration: "Such a rule of action on the part of a governing board contains the potency of grave injury to the institution under its control, not less than of grave injustice to individuals. . . . Just how effective this rule may be, as a means of 'preserving a practical working organization,' is well illustrated by the present condition of the University of Utah." Pointing to the resignation of sixteen members of the faculty in protest of the board's action, the loss of faculty morale, and the light in which the institution had put itself nationally, the committee opined that the board's position "is certain to engender far more 'friction' than it allays; it is not permanently effective even in the management of workshops or business houses. Applied in the government of universities, it is the sure beginning of disaster."[10]

The Utah committee's doubt about whether the exercise of autocratic power was suitable even in the business

world must be understood in the context of the controversy then raging over efforts to reform labor relations in
order to create "industrial democracy."[11] In 1919, John
Leitch published *Man to Man: The Story of Industrial
Democracy.* He argued for the actual translation of the
model of constitutional government into the factory, with a
house of representatives composed of the workers, a senate
of supervisors and managers, and a cabinet of executives,
all three of which would have to concur in the formulation
and execution of plant rules and company policies. Farfetched as it seems today, his idea was widely debated, and
even the usually skeptical Oliver Wendell Holmes found
some merit in it.[12] That same year President Woodrow Wilson addressed Congress about the need for reform in the
"essential matter" of "the genuine democratization of industry, based upon a full recognition of the right of those
who work, in whatever rank, to participate in some organic
way in every decision which directly affects their welfare
and the part they are to play in industry."[13] And in that
same year, Parley Paul Womer, the president of Washburn
College in Topeka, Kansas, dismissed Dr. J. E. Kirkpatrick,
a professor of history and political science, on the ground
that his "agitation" had disturbed the "peace of the college." Womer believed that Kirkpatrick's removal was
"absolutely necessary in the interest of harmony and effective cooperation" between the faculty, administration, and
trustees. The case tested whether faculty members could
be dismissed for demanding a voice in institutional policy.

Professor Kirkpatrick's "agitation" had involved pleading for a faculty salary increase and, more importantly, pressing for an explicit albeit advisory role for the faculty in the governance of the college. Washburn College did not then extend such a role to faculty, and it was strongly resisted by the president, who is reported to have said, "I want you to distinctly understand that I am running this institution." Womer's initial response to the faculty's request for the creation of an advisory committee was to the effect that the college depended for financial support from "men of large financial interests, who would be quick to resent any appearance of 'Bolshevism' in the administration of the college."

In essence, Kirkpatrick was dismissed because he had attempted to bring about what the AAUP investigating committee characterized as a "measure of responsible faculty participation in the government of the institution and in the determination of its educational policies." The committee of investigation seized the occasion to expatiate on what it meant for faculty to be "equal" and "independent" participants in institutions of higher education: "The charge [of 'agitation'] is manifestly one which this Association must regard as not less serious than a charge of unwarrantable restriction of freedom of teaching. If leadership in the attempt to alter existing conditions and to introduce a greater degree of representative government into the organization of a college or university is to be punished by dismissal . . . the processes making for reform in the internal constitution of American colleges are threatened at their point of origin, and the teaching profession is deprived of the right of even urging changes which it may believe to be needful."[14]

In 1927, the University of Louisville dismissed the historian Louis Gottschalk. He had protested the administration's summary dismissal of a colleague and had criticized the educational wisdom of certain policies pursued single-mindedly by the president. The president had threatened to dismiss those faculty members whose "'primary interest [is] in graduate or research work'" in preference to undergraduate instruction and had, over the faculty's objection, given students "capable of playing football" academic credit to which they were not entitled under the college's rules. The president reiterated a demand for "loyalty" toward "the declared purposes of the University." The AAUP committee of investigation used the case to develop the rudiments of a theory of intramural speech. It argued that the need for loyalty could never justify the suppression of "critical discussion by members of a faculty."

The sort of "loyalty" which President Colvin seems to have demanded is not loyalty, but subservience, and somewhat resembles the disciplinary subordination of a company to its lieutenant, or of employees to a foreman. . . . The Committee cannot too strongly condemn the attempt to introduce such a conception of "loyalty" into the administration of a reputable college or university. It is impossible, and rightly so, to suppress critical discussion by members of a faculty, of general or special educational policies, unless that end is accomplished by the simple and drastic means of dismissing that faculty. The attempt to abolish such discussion among the members of the Faculty of the University of Louisville, in the center of a highly civilized community, is not only a deplorable anachronism, but tends to destroy the values which can be created only by patient and tolerant effort, by free and open discussion, and by the gradual increase of a common stock of wisdom, which is incapable of monopolization by any administrative officer.[15]

Six years later an AAUP investigating committee went even further in its report on the dismissal of Professor John A. Rice of the Classics Department of Rollins College by President Hamilton Holt. Like Womer, Holt had taken it upon himself to refashion the college, and, like Womer, he expected cooperation and "harmony" from the faculty. The committee of investigation observed that Holt demanded a greater degree of "like-mindedness than is ordinarily to be found—or to be desired—among any considerable body of adult people of intellectual type." Holt announced an "eight-hour day plan"—a fixed period of class study to be conducted in the presence of the instructor for the entire time. "If there is as much as fifty per cent disagreement between me and any member of the faculty, on what I consider a fundamental matter," Holt was quoted as stating, "either he or I should go." The committee concluded that dismissal for disagreement was "a manifest infringement of academic freedom, though the issue over which it took place was an educational rather than a theological, political, or economic one." The committee explained that "it was not a question of supporting or not supporting the more general and fundamental principles of the College. No teacher having a high degree of professional self-respect is . . . likely to accept service in an institution in which freedom of individual opinion, and the exercise of professional responsibility, on educational matters is denied in the degree which it was denied by President Holt on this occasion."[16]

By 1933, the AAUP had come to view intramural expression as a full-fledged form of academic freedom. If the Washburn committee in 1919 had considered the suppression of intramural speech to be "*not less serious* than a charge of unwarrantable restriction on freedom of teaching," the Rollins College committee branded it "a *manifest infringement of academic freedom.*" The central question was the right of faculty to express independent judgment about matters of institutional policy. The mature view of the AAUP was that faculty ought not to be treated as mere employees whose opinions could be suppressed if they were not sufficiently respectful or loyal. Instead faculty might even have a "professional responsibility" to express their considered views "on educational matters."

The 1940 *Statement*

The 1940 *Statement* does not explicitly refer to freedom of intramural speech. Instead it asserts that "college and university teachers are citizens, members of a learned profession, *and officers of an educational institution.*"[17] The word "officer" supplants the word "appointee" used in

1915, but both are deployed to designate a different status from that of "employee." In effect the 1940 *Statement* embraces the special role for faculty that the 1915 *Declaration* had prophetically imagined.[18]

Freedom of intramural speech follows from this redefinition of the role of faculty. It renders any institutional policy or decision a fair subject for faculty comment or criticism. This freedom has been affirmed and reaffirmed in cases involving the selection of administrators,[19] admission standards,[20] curricular change,[21] athletic policy,[22] land acquisition,[23] and a good deal more.[24] It is a liberty of workplace expression rarely encountered—or tolerated—in the business world. A former president of Princeton University, Harold Dodds, has observed that academic freedom is "a peculiar kind of freedom of a sort which the honest layman does not encounter in his own business or professional experience. Indeed, on the surface it seems to him *to contravene those standards* of responsibility for the interest of colleagues in the organization and *of personal loyalty to the welfare of the institution* which he observes in his ordinary business and professional relationships."[25]

Freedom of intramural expression reflects the special nature of institutions of higher education. Ordinary business organizations serve private economic interests. These interests can be arbitrary or personal. In large publicly owned corporations, these interests are frequently determined by the attribution of rational and predictable profit incentives to shareholders. By law and custom, corporate management is empowered to speak for these interests and to command the execution of policies that will serve them.

It can direct the conduct of employees and suppress criticism of its actions.[26]

Principles of academic freedom, by contrast, presuppose that institutions of higher education serve the public interest and that they promote the common good. The common good is not to be determined by the arbitrary, private, or personal decree of any single individual;[27] nor is it to be determined by the technocratic calculation of rational and predictable profit incentives.[28] The common good is made visible only through open debate and discussion in which all are free to participate. Faculty, by virtue not only of their educational training and expertise but also of their institutional knowledge and commitment, have an indispensable role to play in that debate. Freedom of intramural expression protects this role.[29] It insists that institutions whose mission is to serve the public good are best served by the protection of robust debate and that the corporate management of these institutions, although invested with formal legal authority, cannot define the public good simply by ukase.

Although freedom of intramural expression does not entitle faculty to participate in actual institutional decision making, such an entitlement would be the logical outgrowth of the idea of institutional citizenship on which this aspect of academic freedom rests. By the mid-twentieth century, the 1915 *Declaration*'s long-term project of altering the perception of the role of faculty within colleges and universities had begun to bear tangible fruit in this regard.[30] The rules of many if not most institutions authorized faculty to share in institutional governance.[31] In 1966, after nearly a decade of negotiation, the jointly formulated *Statement on Government of Colleges and Universities* was published.[32] It recognizes the primacy of the faculty's role in fundamental educational matters,[33] but, more importantly for purposes here, it accords faculty a participative, consultative, or information-sharing role in virtually every important area of college and university life.[34]

CHAPTER 6

Freedom of Extramural Expression

The most theoretically problematic aspect of academic freedom is extramural expression. This dimension of academic freedom does not concern communications that are connected to faculty expertise, for such expression is encompassed within freedom of research, a principle that includes both the freedom to inquire and the freedom to disseminate the results of inquiry. Nor does extramural expression concern communications made by faculty in their role as officers of institutions of higher education. Freedom of extramural expression refers instead to speech made by faculty in their capacity as citizens, speech that is typically about matters of public concern and that is unrelated to either scholarly expertise or institutional affiliation. If Scott Chisholm had burned a flag at a public demonstration against the war in Vietnam,[1] or if David Green had burned his draft card at such a protest,[2] they would have engaged in extramural speech. The question is whether and how such speech is protected by academic freedom.

Theoretical Foundations

The question has been troublesome from the beginning. In his 1900 presidential address at the University of Chicago, William Rainey Harper condemned "abuses" of the professorial privilege of freedom of expression. One such abuse was indiscrete extramural speech: "A professor abuses his privilege in many cases when, although shut off in large measure from the world, and engaged within a narrow field of investigation, he undertakes to instruct his colleagues or the public concerning matters in the world at large in connection with which he has had little or no experience. A professor abuses his privilege of freedom of expression of opinion when he fails to exercise that quality, which it must be confessed in some cases the professor lacks, ordinarily called common sense. A professor ought not to make such an exhibition of his weakness or to make an exhibition of his weakness so many times that the attention of the public at large is called to the fact. In this respect he has no larger liberty than other men."[3]

In sharp contrast to its otherwise robust assertion of disciplinary self-confidence, the 1915 *Declaration* was genuinely diffident about extramural speech:

In their extramural utterances, it is obvious that academic teachers are under a peculiar obligation to avoid hasty or unverified or exaggerated statements, and to refrain from intemperate or sensational modes of expression. But, subject to these restraints, it is not, in this committee's opinion, desirable that scholars should be debarred from giving expression to their judgments upon controversial questions, or that their freedom of speech, outside the university, should be limited to questions falling within their own specialties. It is clearly not proper that they should be prohibited from lending their active support to organized movements which they believe to be in the public interest. And, speaking broadly, it may be said in the words of a nonacademic body already once quoted in a publication of this Association, that "it is neither possible nor desirable to deprive a college professor of the political rights vouchsafed to every citizen."

It is, however, a question deserving of consideration by members of the Association, and by university officials, how far academic teachers, at least those dealing with political, economic, and social subjects, should be prominent in the management of our great party organizations, or should be candidates for state or national offices of a distinctly political character. It is manifestly desirable that such teachers have minds untrammeled by party loyalties, unexcited by party enthusiasms, and unbiased by personal political ambitions; and that universities should remain uninvolved in party antagonisms. On the other hand, it is equally manifest that the material available for the service of the state would be restricted in a highly undesirable way, if it were understood that no member of the academic profession should ever be called upon to assume the responsibilities of public office. This question may, in the committee's opinion, suitably be made a topic for special discussion at some future meeting of this Association, in order that a practical policy, which shall do justice to the two partially conflicting considerations that bear upon the matter, may be agreed upon.

The uncertainty of the 1915 *Declaration* was reflected in early Committee A investigations. An example is the case of Professor Arthur Fisher, who had been dismissed by the State Board of Education from his position as a professor of law at the University of Montana in 1921. Fisher was the editor of the *New Northwest,* the newspaper of the Nonpartisan League and the Farmer Labor Party. He was attacked by the American Legion and by the editor of Missoula's morning and evening newspapers, who protested that he was not fit for professorial office. "Academic freedom," the AAUP investigating committee, flatly stated, "is here not directly under consideration." "But," the committee added, "surely no teacher in a republic can be expected to unclothe himself of his interests and activities as a citizen of the State. Participation in outside activities—whether in the service of corporations, political parties, newspapers or churches or in any other field of public interest—should be left to the good judgment of the individual instructor."[4]

Despite these inauspicious beginnings, freedom of extramural expression developed rapidly in the next half century. By the time of the 1940 *Statement,* extramural expression was unambiguously accepted as an essential dimension of academic freedom, although the *Statement* was cautious in describing the extent to which extramural speech was protected: "College and university teachers are citizens, members of a learned profession, and officers of an educational institution. When they speak or write as citizens, they should be free from institutional censorship or discipline, but their special position in the community imposes special obligations. As scholars and educational officers, they should remember that the public may judge their profession and their institution by their utterances. Hence they should at all times be accurate, should exercise appropriate restraint, should show respect for the opinions of others, and should make every effort to indicate that they are not speaking for the institution."[5]

In 1970, the AAUP and the Association of American Colleges authorized a joint and authoritative interpretation of the 1940 *Statement*[6] that removed many of these qualifications: "The controlling principle is that a faculty member's expression of opinion as a citizen cannot constitute grounds for dismissal unless it clearly demonstrates the faculty member's unfitness for his or her position. Extramural utterances rarely bear upon the faculty member's fitness for the position."

The Committee A case law that preceded and subsequently explained this recasting of the 1940 *Statement* is of great interest, and we consider it later in this chapter. At the moment, however, we turn to the larger theoretical question of why extramural expression should be protected as an aspect of *academic* freedom. Why should faculties be free to speak in public in ways that damage their institutions, even if such speech is by hypothesis unprotected by freedom of research or intramural expression?

Arthur Lovejoy, one of the primary authors of the 1915

Declaration, later implied that freedom of extramural expression should be regarded not as an aspect of academic freedom but instead as a kind of general civil liberty: "In some cases teachers have been dismissed or otherwise penalized because of their exercise, outside the university, of their ordinary political or personal freedom in a manner or for purposes objectionable to the governing authorities of their institutions. While such administrative action is contrary to the spirit of academic freedom, it is primarily a special case of the abuse of the economic relation of employer and employee for the denial of ordinary civil liberties."[7] No less a champion of academic freedom than Harvard president Abbott Lawrence Lowell offered a similar analysis, concluding that "the right of a professor to express his views without restraint on matters lying outside the sphere of his professorship" was "not a question of academic freedom in its true sense, but of the personal liberty of the citizen. It has nothing to do with liberty of research and instruction in the subject for which the professor occupies the chair that makes him a member of the university. The fact that a man fills a chair of astronomy, for example, confers on him no special knowledge of, and no peculiar right to speak upon, the protective tariff. His right to speak about a subject on which he is not an authority is simply the right of any other man, and the question is simply whether the university or college by employing him as a professor acquires a right to restrict his freedom as a citizen."[8]

The idea that freedom of extramural expression reflects "ordinary civil liberties" or "the personal liberty of the citizen" is unconvincing. Citizens typically retain civil liberties against government sanctions, not against private authority. Absent specific statutory protections, which are quite rare, courts are extremely reluctant to apply norms of freedom of expression to private work relationships. In the absence of contractual protections, the vast majority of employees have nothing like freedom of extramural expression vis-à-vis their employers.

Employees of the state stand in a somewhat different position. In the years since the 1940 *Statement,* government employees have acquired certain First Amendment rights that protect their ability to speak in public as citizens. Some extramural speech of faculty at public universities is therefore protected by the Constitution.[9] But these protections should not be confused with the profession's understanding of freedom of extramural expression. The First Amendment has been interpreted to allow the regulation of employee speech for broad managerial purposes that afford much deference to "the mission and functions of the [government] employer."[10] The scope of First Amendment rights is accordingly quite limited.[11] Whatever justifications freedom of extramural expression might have, they plainly do not derive from the cribbed constitutional rights of government employees.

Three distinct lines of analysis have been developed to explain why freedom of extramural expression might be included within the principles of academic freedom. The first rests on the premise that it is difficult and dangerous to set artificial limits on faculty expertise, so efforts to distinguish speech within a scholar's competence from speech outside that competence ought to be discouraged. Consider the example of Noam Chomsky. Trained only as a linguist, and hired only to teach linguistics, Chomsky nevertheless continues to write highly controversial publications about foreign policy.[12] To assert that Chomsky's freedom of research can extend only so far as the courses he happens to teach, or only so far as the training he happened to receive, would needlessly inhibit the natural growth and expansion of his academic interests. Seen from this angle, we might argue that the scholarly ambition and form of Chomsky's publications justify their protection as an aspect of his freedom of research.

Something like the Chomsky example arose in 1931 when the Board of Trustees of the Ohio State University dismissed Herbert A. Miller, a professor of sociology, for having spoken at a march sponsored by Mahatma Gandhi in Bombay, India. The board's ostensible ground was that Miller's speech would give offense to the British.[13] (This ground was bad enough, but the AAUP investigating committee found that it was in fact a pretext for the board's dislike of Professor Miller's views on race relations.)[14] Professor Miller was a sociologist of race who had a personal interest in China and India. His remarks show how difficult it can be to separate professional from civic expression:

I feel that it is not right that an American should be asked to speak at this meeting. But I am a professor who is interested in the way human beings are trying to solve their problems. I have spent five years in India and have seen many of the great men of India. I know that the whole world is looking toward that noble experiment which Mahatma Gandhi has started, and they are trying to discover two things. The first is, how much are you interested in the movement and second how will you settle the differences between you.

I feel that this movement is very characteristic of the history of India. For the last five thousand years the great contribution of India has been religion. The thing you are trying to do now is to bring religion to the solution of the two great problems that I have mentioned, namely, the problem of settling your differences in a genuine religious spirit and the problem of applying religion to the solution of practical problems. The success of this movement will be the greatest contribution that India would ever make to human affairs.[15]

The influence of Miller's research and scholarship is plainly evident in his remarks.

The attempt to justify freedom of extramural expression in terms of its intrinsic connection to freedom of research is fraught with conceptual difficulties. It suggests that the very category of extramural expression is superfluous because it is entirely indistinguishable from freedom of research. It also implies that professional standards of care and rigor ought to apply to extramural speech.[16] Expression appropriate to freedom of research contrasts rather sharply with the "uninhibited, robust, and wide-open" speech that characterizes the public debate of citizens.[17] Some such thought seems to lie behind the hedged protections for extramural speech advanced by the 1940 *Statement,* which is alert to the idea that "the public may judge" the profession and higher education on the basis of extramural speech, which must therefore "at all times be accurate" and display "appropriate restraint."

Most fundamentally, it seems implausible to claim that *all* extramural expression by faculty is connected to freedom of research and publication. It may be difficult to draw lines in particular cases, but surely we are not utterly incapable of distinguishing between speech that does and does not express scholarly expertise. Lowell's example of the astronomer who opines on the tariff comes to mind.[18] It seems overwrought to claim that *nothing* is theoretically beyond the legitimate professional expertise of a scholar because the "prolonged and specialized technical training" of the professoriat imparts a methodological rigor that can contribute to the search for knowledge in any and all matters.

The deficiencies of this justification of freedom of extramural expression have prompted a second line of analysis, which focuses on the practical situation of institutions of higher education and the faculty within them. Universities and colleges may penalize politically outspoken professors to appease powerful interests—typically donors, trustees, or state legislatures—who are outraged by faculty expression. Invoking a theme advanced in the 1940 *Statement,* institutions of higher education tend to believe that their reputation and support might suffer if they are associated with an "irresponsible" instructor. They know that in the eyes of the public, universities and colleges are frequently held accountable for the expression of their faculty.

The risk that important constituencies might take offense at faculty speech thus perennially overhangs univer-

sities. The threat persists whether faculty speech constitutes an exercise of professional expertise, and hence is
protected by the fundamental freedom of research and
publication, or whether faculty speech is by contrast unrelated to any professional scholarship, and hence constitutes extramural speech. An example of the former is the
case of Louis Levine, which we discussed in chapter 3.[19]
An example of the latter is the case of William Wickersham, whose signed employment agreement with Columbia College (Missouri) was repudiated by the board of
trustees because he participated in peace demonstrations
at the nearby University of Missouri.[20]

Fundamental principles of academic freedom require
institutions of higher education to resist public pressure to
punish professors like Levine whose research causes public outrage. But it is plain that universities and colleges
would be placed in an extremely awkward position were
they to refuse to discipline speech protected by freedom of
research and publication, but seek to appease public indignation with regard to extramural expression that is unrelated to professional competence, like Wickersham's. In
such circumstances universities and colleges would virtually invite offended constituencies to argue that faculty expression should be censored because it is insufficiently
related to scholarly expertise to merit the protection of
freedom of research.

Institutions of higher education would thus strengthen
their ability to protect freedom of research if they refused
categorically to accept responsibility for the expression of
their faculty, regardless of the precise connection between

such expression and the academic expertise for which faculty have been hired or trained. The advantages of such a categorical rule prompted Abbott Lawrence Lowell to support exactly this rationale for freedom of extramural expression: "If a university or college censors what its professors may say, if it restrains them from uttering something that it does not approve, it thereby assumes responsibility for that which it permits them to say. This is logical and inevitable, but it is a responsibility which an institution of learning would be very unwise in assuming. . . . If a university is right in restraining its professors, it has a duty to do so, and it is responsible for whatever it permits. There is no middle ground. Either the university assumes full responsibility for permitting its professors to express certain opinions in public, or it assumes no responsibility whatever, and leaves them to be dealt with like other citizens by the public authorities according to the laws of the land."[21]

Freedom of extramural expression can on these grounds be defended as a good strategy for minimizing the institutional vulnerability of institutions that must protect freedom of research. Just as universities and colleges disclaim responsibility for the many conflicting contentions of the millions of books that they collect in their libraries, so that no one can plausibly claim that a university supports a geocentric view of the solar system merely because its library contains a copy of Ptolemy, so universities and colleges can disclaim responsibility for the many conflicting political contentions of their faculty, so that no one can plausibly claim that a university supports the Palestinian cause because a computer scientist in its engineering department happens to take that position.[22]

Viewed in this way, however, freedom of extramural expression ceases to constitute a distinct right of academic freedom, but instead finds its justification in counsels of institutional expedience and prudence. Its rationale depends upon wise organizational policy. Those who desire a stronger, more bracing defense of extramural expression have therefore turned to yet a third line of analysis, which stresses the perspective of faculty rather than that of institutional managers.

Beginning with the premise that the experience of freedom is indivisible, this justification of freedom of extramural expression postulates that faculty can promote knowledge or model independent thought in the classroom only if they are *actively* and *imaginatively* engaged in their work. If faculty experience their institutions as repressive, they will be vulnerable to forms of self-censorship and self-restraint that are inconsistent with the confidence necessary for research and teaching. The harm would be enhanced if faculty were confused about which communications were protected by freedom of research and which communications would be exposed to punishment if freedom of extramural speech were not a recognized dimension of academic freedom. Such confusion would be inevitable because the line between academic expertise and extramural expression is unclear, as is illustrated in the examples of Noam Chomsky and Herbert Miller. To suppress extramural speech would thus create an atmosphere of repression inconsistent with the climate of trust and autonomy necessary for faculty to contribute optimally to the mission of higher education.

On this account, freedom of extramural expression is conceptualized as a prophylactic protection for freedom of research and freedom of teaching. Freedom of extramural expression is justified by a practical concern for maintaining conditions conducive to the performance of essential faculty tasks. Of the three justifications for freedom of extramural expression, this is the explanation that recurs most prominently in the case law of Committee A.

Committee A Precedents

An important early case involving freedom of extramural expression under the 1940 *Statement* involved the dismissal of George F. Parker, an assistant professor of religion and philosophy at Evansville College in Indiana.[23] One charge against Parker was that he actively supported Henry Wallace's campaign for the presidency of the United States. Evansville's president, Lincoln B. Hale, had cautioned Parker against assuming the chairmanship of Wallace's county campaign committee. "I made it quite clear," President Hale later wrote, "that further participation in such an official political capacity would prove embarrassing to me and would be certain to seriously harm Evansville College."

On the evening of April 6, 1948, Wallace addressed a large political rally. Professor Parker delivered an invocation (he was an ordained minister of the Baptist Church) and offered a brief talk. The rally was a tumultuous affair, and a vigorous communal clamor for Parker's removal ensued. President Hale acceded to the public demand. The case for removal was put succinctly in a public statement of the college's administrative officers: "Of basic significance is the urban college pattern—the fact that Evansville College is 'closely integrated with the city, whose broad educational need it serves,' and therefore 'is sensitive to the community which values its work and services.' Because of this integration and sensitivity, the conspicuous involvement of a Faculty member in politics is interpreted by the public as involving the College itself; as a result the College loses the general, nonpartisan support of the community, and suffers a loss of influence and effectiveness. A teacher who stands stubbornly upon some theoretical right and disregards the effect upon the College exhibits such a degree of irresponsibility that the College can protect itself only by removing him."

The AAUP investigating committee first addressed the 1940 *Statement*'s requirement that faculty demonstrate "appropriate restraint" in speaking or writing "as citizens." The committee reasoned that the *Statement* could not be interpreted to mean a withdrawal from all political activity disfavored by a college administration, because that would be inconsistent with the *Statement*'s recognition that faculty retained rights of citizenship. Because Parker did no more than publicly support a political candidate, his behavior could not be categorized as failing to demonstrate "appropriate restraint."

The committee recognized a distinction between freedom of teaching and research and freedom of extramural expression, but it claimed that the latter was "of cognate importance": "An institution of higher learning in which freedom of teaching and research do not exist is unworthy of the name, no matter how successful it may have been in community relationships, in fund-raising campaigns, and in other enterprises. For example, if research, reasonably conceived and properly executed, leads to conclusions that are offensive to potent local interests, and arouses hostile criticism, the teacher concerned should expect the support of the institution's administration. *Civic and political freedom for teachers is of cognate importance.*"[24]

The committee's reasoning turned on the indivisibility of freedom within institutions of higher education. The dismissal of Parker threatened "*the loss of freedom,* without which no institution of higher education can fulfill its obligations to the students and to society." The committee drew upon a report by Committee A of the previous year, which had addressed the question whether membership in the Communist Party should be considered per se grounds for dismissal. Committee A concluded that the exclusion of teachers with "unorthodox political views . . . would mean the exclusion of some of the liveliest intellects and most stimulating personalities on our campuses. Furthermore, the acceptance of political discrimination might well be the wolf's paw in the door; such discrimination might presently extend to other types of heterodoxy. Faculty members in general might . . . sagaciously conclude that they cannot afford the luxury of ranging thought and bold speech. Our campuses would then lose the stimulus of clashing opinions and would become havens of cautious mediocrity. Having surrendered its function of criticism and improvement, higher education would retain only its function of preservation and transmission; it would be ready to become an instrument of indoctrination for an authoritarian society."[25]

Faculty are likely to believe that an institution that is quick to suppress unpopular extramural speech is not likely to shield unpopular faculty expression that constitutes genuine research or the exercise of genuine independence in the classroom. An institution inclined to yield to the pressure of its constituencies is not likely to inspire the trust required to sustain the active engagement necessary for faculty to perform their work. The suppression of extramural speech can thus establish an atmosphere of caution and fear that is inconsistent with the fulfillment of the academic mission to promote new knowledge and to model independent thought. That, at least, was the conclusion of Committee A, which, reflecting on the firing of Parker, declared that the suppression of political action "cannot be confined to nonacademic activities; and unless we adhere to the principles of freedom it will inevitably manifest itself in scholarship and will reduce learning to dogmatism." Committee A explained:

When the Administration of a college or university represses a political activity which contravenes dominant local opinions, it thereby lends its support to the establishment of those opinions. The institution that travels far in this direction is soon reduced, in so far as it is effective at all, to the role of serving as an agency of indoctrination in the views of some group or party. When it begins, in the face of local pressures, to yield its functions as a guardian of freedom, it does more than restrict political freedom; it inevitably curtails its capacity to foster the search for truth, and to that extent contributes to shape itself into the pattern of those who regard the truth as already fully known. It matters not whether the field be that of political action, or of research and teaching in science, politics, religion, or social theory; youth seeking a proper education in a changing world needs to repair to places where there is courage to face what the seekers may find and what the future may unfold. This courage will not long survive among those who are terrorized or repressed in their political and civic lives.[26]

Committee A's commitment to this principle underlies the important series of cases in which it sought to clarify the meaning of the many qualifications that the 1940 *Statement* imposed on extramural expression. As we have noted, the *Statement* provides that faculty "should remember that the public may judge their profession and their institution by their utterances. Hence they should at all times be accurate, should exercise appropriate restraint, should show respect for the opinions of others, and should make every effort to indicate that they are not speaking for the institution." The meaning of these reservations came to a head in the dismissal of Leo Koch, an assistant professor of biology at the University of Illinois, in 1960.[27] The student newspaper had published an article about sex on the campus. This prompted Professor Koch to write a letter to the editor condemning Victorian prudery and religious Puritanism: "With modern contraceptives and medical advice readily available at the nearest drugstore, or at least a family physician, there is no valid reason why sexual intercourse should not be condoned among those sufficiently mature to engage in it without social consequences and without violating their own codes of morality and ethics."

The letter was condemned straightaway by the university's president, who ordered Koch's termination. The matter was heard by the faculty senate, which recommended a reprimand in lieu of discharge but which argued that the letter was a breach of academic responsibility because its manner of expression was inimical to the standing of the university in the eyes of the people of Illinois. The matter was later heard by the board of trustees, which found the "language, tone, and contents of the letter" a "reprehensible breach of . . . academic and professional responsibility" and "prejudicial to the best interests" of the university. The board discharged Koch.

The AAUP investigating committee, chaired by Thomas I. Emerson of Yale Law School, reviewed the history of the 1940 *Statement* and concluded that the reservations of the 1940 *Statement* were only hortatory.[28] Its interpretation of the *Statement* was consistent with a 1956 AAUP report titled *Academic Freedom and Tenure in the Quest for National Security,* which had concluded that the mere refusal of a faculty member to account for his political beliefs or associations to a congressional committee or to his home institution could not be considered a sufficient cause for dismissal. The touchstone must instead be fitness for office: "Removal can be justified only on the ground, established by evidence, of unfitness to teach because of incompetence, lack of scholarly objectivity or integrity, serious misuse of the classroom or of academic prestige, gross personal misconduct, or conscious participation in conspiracy against the government. The same principle applies, *a fortiori*, to alleged involvement in Communist-inspired activities or views."[29] This conclusion implied that faculty could not be penalized for extramural expression unless their speech also evidenced unfitness for the tasks of research, teaching, or institutional citizenship.

This same conclusion underlay the investigating committee's interpretation of the 1940 *Statement* in the Koch case. Notwithstanding its earlier pronouncements, Committee A was unwilling to endorse this understanding of the 1940 *Statement*, although it was willing to authorize publication of the investigating committee's report.[30] The investigating committee was vindicated in 1970 when the AAUP, together with the Association of American Colleges, issued what is now the definitive interpretation of the 1940 *Statement*. That interpretation expressly provides that "the controlling principle is that a faculty member's expression of opinion as a citizen cannot constitute grounds for dismissal unless it clearly demonstrates the faculty member's unfitness for his or her position. Extramural utterances rarely bear upon the faculty member's fitness for the position."

The significance of this interpretation of the 1940 *State-*

ment was explicated in the investigation of one of the most contentious campus controversies of the latter part of the twentieth century—the decision of the Board of Regents of the University of California to relieve the president of the university and the chancellor of the Los Angeles campus of any responsibility in the matter of the reappointment of Angela Davis as acting assistant professor of philosophy and itself to issue her notice of nonrenewal of appointment. The basis for the board's unprecedented action was a series of four public speeches that the regents concluded were "so extreme, so antithetical to the protection of academic freedom and so obviously deliberately false in several respects" as to be disqualifying.

The AAUP investigating committee attended to the idea of *fitness.* "The faculty member's shortcoming must be shown to bear some identified relation to his capacity or willingness to perform the responsibilities, broadly conceived, to his students, to his colleagues, to his discipline, or to the functions of his institution, that pertain to his assignment. The concept cannot be reduced to a generalized judgment of 'unsuitability' at large. AAUP standards of responsibility identify objectionable features in extramural speech, and their presence in any serious degree is prima facie evidence to trigger an inquiry into the speaker's fitness for an academic position, *but it does not by itself establish unfitness.*" The committee linked the concept of fitness to professional self-regulation, arguing that faculty, who were experts in scholarly standards and norms, were better able to judge fitness than a lay board of regents: "Academic judges may have a higher tolerance for verbal contention, however farfetched or indiscreet, for reasons that go beyond mere guild loyalty; but they may be more concerned with evidence of charlatanism or overall quality in the speaker's total academic performance. Presumably, on the other hand, controversial extramural utterance will be of concern to a lay governing board precisely to the extent that it is a matter of public rather than academic controversy. To that extent, the judgment of such a board under an identical general standard is likely to focus on those aspects of the total conduct that outrage public sensibilities and to undervalue those that relate to professional performance within the academic discipline."[31]

The upshot of this reasoning is that extramural speech cannot be disciplined unless it bears on professional competence, and judgments of professional competence, for reasons we have discussed, are primarily reserved for faculty determination.[32] Because principles of academic freedom obligate faculty to observe norms of professional competence, regulating extramural expression in this way cannot chill the freedoms necessary for faculty engagement. Faculty can concentrate on fulfilling their professional responsibilities rather than worry about offending public constituencies. This has been the theory of extramural expression advanced by Committee A for the past many decades.

CHAPTER 7

Conclusion

On Professional Responsibility

Academic freedom is not the freedom to speak or to teach just as one wishes. It is the freedom to pursue the scholarly profession, inside and outside the classroom, according to the norms and standards of that profession.

The 1915 *Declaration* perceived three primary threats to this freedom. The first concerned an ecclesiastical orthodoxy that sought to restrict professional autonomy in the interests of religious truth. This threat has abated with the decline in the proportion of religiously affiliated institutions in higher education[1] and with the spread of the secular ideals of the 1940 *Statement,* even among church-related institutions.[2]

The second threat involved the prerogatives of "vested interests" who claimed that their financial support of institutions of higher education carried with it the right to demand conformity with their own particular views. Although this quasi-proprietary claim is not trumpeted today as it was a century ago, it has revived in a new, more subtle, but no less dangerous, form. Donors may no longer claim the prerogative to proscribe dissent, but they may assert the right to prescribe the content of the programs they fund.[3] The ravenous need for financial resources has driven universities to encourage research investment by private corporations, which, predictably, will seek to control the direction and dissemination of university research. Derek Bok has not been alone in warning that universities must remain especially vigilant to ensure that this mounting dependence does not seriously undermine professorial and institutional autonomy.[4]

The third threat was pervasive and ineradicable. The drafters of the 1915 *Declaration* feared most of all what they called "the tyranny of public opinion." They recognized "the tendency of modern democracy . . . for men to think alike, to feel alike, and to speak alike," and they were apprehensive that "any departure from the conventional standards is apt to be regarded with suspicion." The 1915 *Declaration* identified a structural paradox: in a democracy, all institutions of higher education must ultimately depend on popular support, yet faculty cannot pursue new knowledge or instill independence of mind if they are bound by the pieties of public opinion. This paradox persists. We have seen it illustrated time and again in this volume. Arthur Fisher was dismissed in 1921 for offending the American Legion;[5] George Parker was dismissed in

1948 for espousing leftist political beliefs unacceptable in a small Midwestern community;[6] Scott Chisholm was dismissed in 1967 for antagonizing patriotic sensibilities statewide.[7] The paradox is just as relevant for us now as it was in 1915.

Public opinion threatens the autonomy of the scholarly profession in many ways. The raw political force of state legislatures can directly regulate and punish.[8] When Louis Levine was suspended by the University of Montana in 1919, it was on the ground that his publication "would alienate certain friends of the University in the state legislature, and prevent the expected and needed appropriation."[9] When the Ohio State University dismissed Herbert A. Miller in 1931, the AAUP investigating committee noted that "with trustees appointed by the governor, with three trustees out of seven resident in [Columbus], constantly under the eye of the Legislature to which it must apply for its support, the University experiences difficulty in maintaining that detachment from political influences and popular prejudices in which its scholarly work and educational activities can be most effectively pursued."[10]

Even without the direct intervention of elected officials, public opinion powerfully influences the decisions of university administrators. They know that unpopular faculty can arouse the disapproval of alumni, donors, parents, and other significant groups. The AAUP committee investigating the 1934 dismissal of Ralph E. Turner reported that the chancellor of the University of Pittsburgh "was extremely sensitive to criticism of whatever nature if it came from possible donors or would tend in any way to jeopardize the

completion" of the "Cathedral of Learning," a large building project upon which the Chancellor had set his heart.[11]
University administrators "frequently admonished the faculty not to say things that might antagonize 'influential
people.'"[12] In 1949 Rocky Mountain College terminated
the contract of Professor Myron L. Tripp because "'fear was
expressed' that his retention 'would make it more difficult
to solicit funds . . . from conservative businessmen,'" and
administrators believed that it was necessary for Tripp to
go "in order that donations would come in and peace be restored."[13]

The profession of scholarship requires public support,
yet it must also remain independent from public opinion.
This dilemma is difficult to negotiate and always tempting
to resolve in ways incompatible with basic principles of
academic freedom. Consider, for example, Nicholas Murray Butler, who presided over Columbia University for
over forty-three years.[14] Butler understood one side of the
dilemma. He keenly appreciated the force of public opinion, proclaiming that scholars owed "a decent respect to
the opinions of mankind. Men who feel that their personal
convictions require them to treat the mature opinion of the
civilized world without respect or with active contempt
may well be given an opportunity to do so from private station and without the added influence and prestige of a university's name." He believed that faculty ought to behave
"like gentlemen" and use their freedom "responsibly."[15]

Appeals to "responsibility" and "restraint" are typical of
those who perceive the dependence of higher education on
"the opinions of mankind." Thus the Commission on Aca-

demic Freedom and Tenure of the Association of American Colleges asserted in 1922: "Academic freedom is not a myth, neither is it license unrestrained and irresponsible. What it should be may be stated best in terms of liberty and *responsibility.* The ideal college atmosphere is one in which, on the one hand, the institution guarantees to all its teachers unrestricted freedom in teaching, investigation, and publication, and in which, on the other hand, competent, judicious scholars exercise their freedom *with fitting regard for the welfare and reputation of the institution they serve.* Such an atmosphere should be the ultimate aim of learning; in it every trace of the problem of academic freedom would disappear."[16]

"Responsibility" and "restraint" figure prominently and dubiously as standards of conduct in the annals of American academic freedom.[17] The administration of Evansville College, when it dismissed George Parker, proclaimed that "a teacher who stands stubbornly upon some theoretical right and disregards the effect upon the College exhibits such a degree of irresponsibility that the College can protect itself only by removing him."[18] The administration of Indiana State University, when it dismissed Scott Chisholm, argued that Chisholm had failed to "exercise appropriate restraint and show respect for the beliefs, opinions and attitudes of others."[19] Refusing in 1958 to reappoint assistant professor of economics Bud R. Hutchinson because he had published a letter to the college newspaper criticizing its opposition to integration, the administration of Alabama Polytechnic Institute concluded that Hutchinson had failed to exercise "appropriate restraint" and to "show respect for the opinions of others" and that he had thus been "'irresponsible' and flouted the 'known opinion of the administration.'"[20] In 2007 a report focusing on campus debate involving Israeli-Palestinian issues called for "a responsibilities-based approach to upholding academic freedom."[21]

Appeals to responsibility and restraint are no doubt rhetorically effective, but great care must be taken to define the meaning of these terms precisely. Throughout this volume we have stressed that academic responsibility and restraint are indeed required by academic freedom, because academic freedom is the right to pursue a scholar's profession according to the norms of that profession and faculty can accordingly be held accountable for compliance with these norms.[22] But there is a fundamental distinction between holding faculty accountable to professional norms and holding them accountable to public opinion.[23] The former exemplifies academic freedom; the latter undermines it. Even though institutions of higher education in fact depend on public acceptance, they cannot shackle scholars to the "generally accepted beliefs" of those "persons, private or official, through whom society provides the means for the maintenance of universities."[24] Used in the wrong way, catchphrases of responsibility and restraint can "become a negation, rather than a complement, of academic freedom."[25]

The architects of the American idea of academic freedom were well aware of this danger.[26] They knew both that faculty should be professionally responsible and that professional responsibility should be insulated from the pieties of public opinion. They knew both that institutions of higher education would be dependent on public support and that the creation of new knowledge and the pedagogical inculcation of a mature independence of mind required professional autonomy from "the tyranny of public opinion." They devoted their most astute and incisive efforts to the task of bequeathing us a principled tradition in which this fragile autonomy could be maintained. They called it academic freedom.

Excerpts from the 1915 *Declaration of Principles on Academic Freedom and Academic Tenure*

The term "academic freedom" has traditionally had two applications—to the freedom of the teacher and to that of the student, *Lehrfreiheit* and *Lernfreiheit*. It need scarcely be pointed out that the freedom which is the subject of this report is that of the teacher. Academic freedom in this sense comprises three elements: freedom of inquiry and research; freedom of teaching within the university or college; and freedom of extramural utterance and action. The first of these is almost everywhere so safeguarded that the dangers of its infringement are slight. It may therefore be disregarded in this report. The second and third phases of academic freedom are closely related, and are often not distinguished. The third, however, has an importance of its own, since of late it has perhaps more frequently been the occasion of difficulties and controversies than has the question of freedom of intra-academic teaching. All five of the cases which have recently been investigated by committees of this Association have involved, at least as one factor, the right of university teachers to express their opinions freely outside the university or to engage in political activities in their capacity as citizens. The general principles which have to do with freedom of teaching in both these senses seem to the committee to be in great part, though not wholly, the same. In this report, therefore, we shall consider the matter primarily with reference to freedom of teaching within the university, and shall assume that what is said thereon is also applicable to the freedom of speech of university teachers outside their institutions, subject to certain qualifications and supplementary considerations which will be pointed out in the course of the report.

An adequate discussion of academic freedom must necessarily consider three matters: (1) the scope and basis of the power exercised by those bodies having ultimate legal authority in academic affairs; (2) the nature of the academic calling; and (3) the function of the academic institution or university.

1. Basis of Academic Authority

American institutions of learning are usually controlled by boards of trustees as the ultimate repositories of power. Upon them finally it devolves to determine the measure of academic freedom which is to be realized in the several institutions. It therefore becomes necessary to inquire into the nature of the trust reposed in these boards, and to ascertain to whom the trustees are to be considered accountable.

The simplest case is that of a proprietary school or college designed for the propagation of specific doctrines prescribed by those who have furnished its endowment. It is evident that in such cases the trustees are bound by the deed of gift, and, whatever be their own views, are obligated to carry out the terms of the trust. If a church or religious denomination establishes a college to be governed by a board of trustees, with the express understanding that the college will be used as an instrument of propaganda in the interests of the religious faith professed by the church or denomination creating it, the trustees have a right to demand that everything be subordinated to that end. If, again, as has happened in this country, a wealthy manufacturer establishes a special school in a university in order to teach, among other things, the advantages of a protective tariff, or if, as is also the case, an institution has been endowed for the purpose of propagating the doctrines of socialism, the situation is analogous. All of these are essentially proprietary institutions, in the moral sense. They do not, at least as regards one particular subject, accept the principles of freedom of inquiry, of opinion, and of teaching; and their purpose is not to advance knowledge by the unrestricted research and unfettered discussion of impartial investigators, but rather to subsidize the promotion of opinions held by the persons, usually not of the scholar's calling, who provide the funds for their maintenance.

Concerning the desirability of the existence of such institutions, the committee does not wish to express any opinion. But it is manifestly important that they should not be permitted to sail under false colors. Genuine boldness and thoroughness of inquiry, and freedom of speech, are scarcely reconcilable with the prescribed inculcation of a particular opinion upon a controverted question.

Such institutions are rare, however, and are becoming ever more rare. We still have, indeed, colleges under denominational auspices; but very few of them impose upon their trustees responsibility for the spread of specific doctrines. They are more and more coming to occupy, with respect to the freedom enjoyed by the members of their teaching bodies, the position of untrammeled institutions of learning, and are differentiated only by the natural influence of their respective historic antecedents and traditions.

Leaving aside, then, the small number of institutions of the proprietary type, what is the nature of the trust reposed in the governing boards of the ordinary institutions of learning? Can colleges and universities that are not strictly bound by their founders to a propagandist duty ever be included in the class of institutions that we have just described as being in a moral sense proprietary? The answer is clear. If the former class of institutions constitutes a private or proprietary trust, the latter constitutes a public trust. The trustees are trustees for the public. In the case of our state universities this is self-evident. In the case of most of our privately endowed institutions, the situation is really not different. They cannot be permitted to assume the proprietary attitude and privilege, if they are appealing to the general public for support. Trustees of such universities or colleges have no moral right to bind the reason or the conscience of any professor. All claim to such right is waived by the appeal to the general public for contributions and for moral support in the maintenance, not of a propaganda, but of a non-partisan institution of learning. It follows that any university which lays restrictions upon the intellectual freedom of its professors proclaims itself a proprietary institution, and should be so described whenever it makes a general appeal for funds; and the public should be advised that the institution has no claim whatever to general support or regard.

This elementary distinction between a private and a public trust is not yet so universally accepted as it should be in our American institutions. While in many universities and colleges the situation has come to be entirely satisfactory, there are others in which the relation of trustees to professors is apparently still conceived to be analogous to that of a private employer to his employees; in which, therefore, trustees are not regarded as debarred by any moral restrictions, beyond their own sense of expediency, from imposing their personal opinions upon the teaching of the institution, or even from employing the power of dismissal to gratify their private antipathies or resentments. An eminent university president thus described the situation not many years since:

> In the institutions of higher education the board of trustees is the body on whose discretion, good feeling, and experience the securing of academic freedom now depends. There

are boards which leave nothing to be desired in these respects; but there are also numerous bodies that have everything to learn with regard to academic freedom. These barbarous boards exercise an arbitrary power of dismissal. They exclude from the teachings of the university unpopular or dangerous subjects. In some states they even treat professors' positions as common political spoils; and all too frequently, in both state and endowed institutions, they fail to treat the members of the teaching staff with that high consideration to which their functions entitle them.

It is, then, a prerequisite to a realization of the proper measure of academic freedom in American institutions of learning, that all boards of trustees should understand—as many already do—the full implications of the distinction between private proprietorship and a public trust.

2. The Nature of the Academic Calling

The above-mentioned conception of a university as an ordinary business venture, and of academic teaching as a purely private employment, manifests also a radical failure to apprehend the nature of the social function discharged by the professional scholar. While we should be reluctant to believe that any large number of educated persons suffer from such a misapprehension, it seems desirable at this time to restate clearly the chief reasons, lying in the nature of the university teaching profession, why it is in the public interest that the professorial office should be one both of dignity and of independence.

If education is the cornerstone of the structure of society

and if progress in scientific knowledge is essential to civilization, few things can be more important than to enhance the dignity of the scholar's profession, with a view to attracting into its ranks men of the highest ability, of sound learning, and of strong and independent character. This is the more essential because the pecuniary emoluments of the profession are not, and doubtless never will be, equal to those open to the more successful members of other professions. It is not, in our opinion, desirable that men should be drawn into this profession by the magnitude of the economic rewards which it offers; but it is for this reason the more needful that men of high gift and character should be drawn into it by the assurance of an honorable and secure position, and of freedom to perform honestly and according to their own consciences the distinctive and important function which the nature of the profession lays upon them.

That function is to deal at first hand, after prolonged and specialized technical training, with the sources of knowledge; and to impart the results of their own and of their fellow-specialists' investigations and reflection, both to students and to the general public, without fear or favor. The proper discharge of this function requires (among other things) that the university teacher shall be exempt from any pecuniary motive or inducement to hold, or to express, any conclusion which is not the genuine and uncolored product of his own study or that of fellow specialists. Indeed, the proper fulfillment of the work of the professoriate requires that our universities shall be so free that no fair-minded person shall find any excuse for even a suspicion that the utterances of university teachers are shaped or restricted by the judgment, not of professional scholars, but of inexpert and possibly not wholly disinterested persons outside of their ranks. The lay public is under no compulsion to accept or to act upon the opinions of the scientific experts whom, through the universities, it employs. But it is highly needful, in the interest of society at large, that what purport to be the conclusions of men trained for, and dedicated to, the quest for truth, shall in fact be the conclusions of such men, and not echoes of the opinions of the lay public, or of the individuals who endow or manage universities. To the degree that professional scholars, in the formation and promulgation of their opinions, are, or by the character of their tenure appear to be, subject to any motive other than their own scientific conscience and a desire for the respect of their fellow experts, to that degree the university teaching profession is corrupted; its proper influence upon public opinion is diminished and vitiated; and society at large fails to get from its scholars, in an unadulterated form, the peculiar and necessary service which it is the office of the professional scholar to furnish.

These considerations make still more clear the nature of the relationship between university trustees and members of university faculties. The latter are the appointees, but not in any proper sense the employees, of the former. For, once appointed, the scholar has professional functions to perform in which the appointing authorities have neither competency nor moral right to intervene. The responsibility of the university teacher is primarily to the public itself, and to the judgment of his own profession; and while, with respect to certain external conditions of his vocation, he accepts a responsibility to the authorities of the institution in which he serves, in the essentials of his professional activity his duty is to the wider public to which the institution itself is morally amenable. So far as the university teacher's independence of thought and utterance is concerned—though not in other regards—the relationship of professor to trustees may be compared to that between judges of the federal courts and the executive who appoints them. University teachers should be understood to be, with respect to the conclusions reached and expressed by them, no more subject to the control of the trustees than are judges subject to the control of the president with respect to their decisions; while of course, for the same reason, trustees are no more to be held responsible for, or to be presumed to agree with, the opinions or utterances of professors than the president can be assumed to approve of all the legal reasonings of the courts. A university is a great and indispensable organ of the higher life of a civilized community, in the work of which the trustees hold an essential and highly honorable place, but in which the faculties hold an independent place, with quite equal responsibilities—and in relation to purely scientific and educational questions, the primary responsibility. Misconception or obscurity in this matter has undoubtedly been a source of occasional difficulty in the past, and even in several instances during the current year, however much, in the main, a long tradition of kindly and courteous intercourse between trustees and members of university faculties has kept the question in the background.

3. The Function of the Academic Institution

The importance of academic freedom is most clearly perceived in the light of the purposes for which universities exist. These are three in number:

(a) to promote inquiry and advance the sum of human knowledge;
(b) to provide general instruction to the students; and
(c) to develop experts for various branches of the public service.

Let us consider each of these. In the earlier stages of a nation's intellectual development, the chief concern of educational institutions is to train the growing generation and to diffuse the already accepted knowledge. It is only slowly that there comes to be provided in the highest institutions of learning the opportunity for the gradual wresting from nature of her intimate secrets. The modern university is becoming more and more the home of scientific research. There are three fields of human inquiry in which the race is only at the beginning: natural science, social science, and philosophy and religion, dealing with the relations of man to outer nature, to his fellow men, and to ultimate realities and values. In natural science all that we have learned but serves to make us realize more deeply how much more remains to be discovered. In social science in its largest sense, which is concerned with the relations of men in society and with the conditions of social order and well-being, we have learned only an adumbration of the laws which govern these vastly complex phenomena. Finally, in the spirit[ual] life, and in the interpretation of the general meaning and ends of human existence and its relation to the universe, we are still far from a comprehension of the final truths, and from a universal agreement among all sincere and earnest men. In all of these domains of knowledge, the first condition of progress is complete and unlimited freedom to pursue inquiry and publish its results. Such freedom is the breath in the nostrils of all scientific activity.

The second function—which for a long time was the only function—of the American college or university is to provide instruction for students. It is scarcely open to question that freedom of utterance is as important to the teacher as it is to the investigator. No man can be a successful teacher unless he enjoys the respect of his students, and their confidence in his intellectual integrity. It is clear, however, that this confidence will be impaired if there is suspicion on the part of the student that the teacher is not expressing himself fully or frankly, or that college and university teachers in general are a repressed and intimidated class who dare not speak with that candor and courage which youth always demands in those whom it is to esteem. The average student is a discerning observer, who soon takes the measure of his instructor. It is not only the character of the instruction but also the character of the instructor that counts; and if the student has reason to believe that the instructor is not true to himself, the virtue of the instruction as an educative force is incalculably diminished. There must be in the mind of the teacher no mental reservation. He must give the student the best of what he has and what he is.

The third function of the modern university is to develop experts for the use of the community. If there is one thing that distinguishes the more recent developments of democracy, it is the recognition by legislators of the inherent complexities of economic, social, and political life, and the difficulty of solving problems of technical adjustment without technical knowledge. The recognition of this fact has led to a continually greater demand for the aid of experts in these subjects, to advise both legislators and administrators. The training of such experts has, accordingly, in recent years, become an important part of the work of the universities; and in almost every one of our higher institutions of learning the professors of the economic, social, and political sciences have been drafted to an increasing extent into more or less unofficial participation in the public service. It is obvious that here again the scholar must be absolutely free not only to pursue his investigations but to declare the results of his researches, no matter where they may lead him or to what extent they may come into conflict with accepted opinion. To be of use to the legislator or the administrator, he must enjoy their complete confidence in the disinterestedness of his conclusions.

It is clear, then, that the university cannot perform its threefold function without accepting and enforcing to the fullest extent the principle of academic freedom. The responsibility of the university as a whole is to the community at large, and any restriction upon the freedom of the instructor is bound to react injuriously upon the efficiency and the *morale* of the institution, and therefore ultimately upon the interests of the community.

The attempted infringements of academic freedom at present are probably not only of less frequency than, but of a different character from, those to be found in former times. In the early period of university development in America the chief menace to academic freedom was ecclesiastical, and the disciplines chiefly affected were philosophy and the natural sciences. In more recent times the danger zone has been shifted to the political and social sciences—though we still have sporadic examples of the former class of cases in some of our smaller institutions. But it is precisely in these provinces of knowledge in which academic freedom is now most likely to be threatened, that the need for it is at the same time most evident. No person of intelligence believes that all of our political problems have been solved, or that the final stage of social evolution has been reached. Grave issues in the adjustment of men's social and economic relations are certain to call for settlement in the years that are to come; and for the right settlement of them mankind will need all the wisdom, all the good will, all the soberness of mind, and all the knowledge drawn from experience, that it can command. Toward this settlement the university has potentially its own very great contribution to make; for if the adjustment reached is to be a wise one, it must take due account of economic science, and be guided by that breadth of historic vision which it should be one of the functions of a university to cultivate. But if the universities are to render any such service toward the right solution of the social problems of the future, it is the first essential that the scholars who carry on the work of universities shall not be in a position of dependence upon the favor of any social class or group, that the disinterestedness and impartiality of their inquiries and their conclusions shall be, so far as is humanly possible, beyond the reach of suspicion.

The special dangers to freedom of teaching in the domain of the social sciences are evidently two. The one which is the more likely to affect the privately endowed colleges and universities is the danger of restrictions upon the expression of opinions which point toward extensive social innovations, or call in question the moral legitimacy or social expediency of economic conditions or commercial practices in which large vested interests are involved. In the political, social, and economic field almost every question, no matter how large and general it at first appears, is more or less affected by private or class interests; and, as the governing body of a university is naturally made up of men who through their standing and ability are personally interested in great private enterprises, the points of possible conflict are numberless. When to this is added the consideration that benefactors, as well as most of the parents who send their children to privately endowed institutions, themselves belong to the more prosperous and therefore usually to the more conservative classes, it is apparent that, so long as effectual safeguards for academic freedom are not established, there is a real danger that pressure from vested interests may, sometimes deliberately and sometimes unconsciously, sometimes openly and sometimes subtly and in obscure ways, be brought to bear upon academic authorities.

On the other hand, in our state universities the danger may be the reverse. Where the university is dependent for funds upon legislative favor, it has sometimes happened that the conduct of the institution has been affected by political considerations; and where there is a definite governmental policy or a strong public feeling on economic, social, or political questions, the menace to academic freedom may consist in the repression of opinions that in the particular political situation are deemed ultra-conservative rather than ultra-radical. The essential point, however, is not so much that the opinion is of one or another shade, as that it differs from the views entertained by the authorities. The question resolves itself into one of departure from accepted standards; whether the departure is in the one direction or the other is immaterial.

This brings us to the most serious difficulty of this problem; namely, the dangers connected with the existence in a democracy of an overwhelming and concentrated public opinion. The tendency of modern democracy is for men to think alike, to feel alike, and to speak alike. Any departure from the conventional standards is apt to be regarded with suspicion. Public opinion is at once the chief safeguard of a democracy, and the chief menace to the real liberty of the individual. It almost seems as if the danger of despotism cannot be wholly averted under any form of government. In a political autocracy there is no effective public opinion, and all are subject to the tyranny of the ruler; in a democracy there is political freedom, but there is likely to be a tyranny of public opinion.

An inviolable refuge from such tyranny should be found in the university. It should be an intellectual experiment station, where new ideas may germinate and where their fruit, though still distasteful to the community as a whole, may be allowed to ripen until finally, perchance, it may become a part of the accepted intellectual food of the nation or of the world. Not less is it a distinctive duty of the university to be the conservator of all genuine elements of value in the past thought and life of mankind which are not in the fashion of the moment. Though it need not be the "home of beaten causes," the university is, indeed, likely always to exercise a certain form of conservative influence. For by its nature it is committed to the principle that knowledge should precede action, to the caution (by no means synonymous with intellectual timidity) which is an essential part of the scientific method, to a sense of the complexity of social problems, to the practice of taking long views into the future, and to a reasonable regard for the teachings of experience. One of its most characteristic functions in a democratic society is to help make public opinion more self-critical and more circumspect, to check the more hasty and unconsidered impulses of popular feeling, to train the democracy to the habit of looking before and after. It is precisely this function of the university which is most injured by any restriction upon academic freedom; and it is precisely those who most value this aspect of the university's work who should most earnestly protest against any such restriction. For the public may respect, and be influenced by, the counsels of prudence and of moderation which are given by men of science, if it believes those counsels to be the disinterested expression of the scientific temper and of unbiased inquiry. It is little likely to respect or heed them if it has reason to believe that they are the expression of the interests, or the timidities, of the limited portion of the community which is in a position to endow institutions of learning, or is most likely to be represented upon their boards of trustees. And a plausible reason for this belief is given the public so long as our universities are not organized in such a way as to make impossible any exercise of pressure upon professorial opinions and utterances by governing boards of laymen.

Since there are no rights without corresponding duties, the considerations heretofore set down with respect to the freedom of the academic teacher entail certain correlative obligations. The claim to freedom of teaching is made in the interest of the integrity and of the progress of scientific inquiry; it is, therefore, only those who carry on their work in the temper of the scientific inquirer who may justly assert this claim. The liberty of the scholar within the university to set forth his conclusions, be they what they may, is conditioned by their being conclusions gained by a scholar's method and held in a scholar's spirit; that is to say, they must be the fruits of competent and patient and sincere inquiry, and they should be set forth with dignity, courtesy, and temperateness of language. The university teacher, in giving instruction upon controversial matters, while he is under no obligation to hide his own opinion under a mountain of equivocal verbiage, should, if he is fit for his position, be a person of a fair and judicial mind; he should, in dealing with such subjects, set forth justly, without suppression or innuendo, the divergent opinions of other investigators; he should cause his students to become familiar with the best published expressions of the great historic types of doctrine upon the questions at issue; and he should, above all, remember that his business is not to provide his students with ready-made conclusions, but to train them to think for themselves, and to provide them access to those materials which they need if they are to think intelligently.

It is, however, for reasons which have already been made evident, inadmissible that the power of determining when departures from the requirements of the scientific spirit and method have occurred, should be vested in bodies not composed of members of the academic profession. Such bodies necessarily lack full competency to judge of those requirements; their intervention can never be exempt from the suspicion that it is dictated by other motives than zeal for the integrity of science; and it is, in any case, unsuitable to the dignity of a great profession that the initial responsibility for the maintenance of its professional standards should not be in the hands of its own members. It follows that university teachers must be prepared to assume this responsibility for themselves. They have hitherto seldom had the opportunity, or perhaps the disposition, to do so. The obligation will doubtless, therefore, seem to many an unwelcome and burdensome one; and for its proper discharge members of the profession will perhaps need to acquire, in a greater measure than they at present possess it, the capacity for impersonal judgment in such cases, and for judicial severity when the occasion requires it. But the responsibility cannot, in this committee's opinion, be rightfully evaded. If this profession should prove itself unwilling to purge its ranks of the incompetent and the unworthy, or to prevent the freedom which it claims in the name of science from being used as a shelter for inefficiency, for superficiality, or for uncritical and intemperate partisanship, it is certain that the task will be performed by others—by others who lack certain essential qualifications for performing it, and whose action is sure to breed suspicions and recurrent controversies deeply injurious to the internal order and the public standing of universities. Your committee has, therefore, in the appended "Practical Proposals," attempted to suggest means by which judicial action by representatives of the profession, with respect to the matters here referred to, may be secured.

There is one case in which the academic teacher is under an obligation to observe certain special restraints— namely, the instruction of immature students. In many of our American colleges, and especially in the first two years of the course, the student's character is not yet fully formed, his mind is still relatively immature. In these circumstances it may reasonably be expected that the instructor will present scientific truth with discretion, that he will introduce the student to new conceptions gradually, with some consideration for the student's preconceptions and traditions, and with due regard to character-building. The teacher ought also to be especially on his guard against taking unfair advantage of the student's immaturity by indoctrinating him with the teacher's own opinions before the student has had an opportunity fairly to examine other opinions upon the matters in question, and before he has sufficient knowledge and ripeness of judgment to be entitled to form any definitive opinion of his own. It is not the least service which a college or university may render to those under its instruction, to habituate them to looking not only patiently but methodically on both sides, before adopting any conclusion upon controverted issues. By these suggestions, however, it need scarcely be said that the committee does not intend to imply that it is not the duty of an academic instructor to give to any students old enough to be in college a genuine intellectual awakening and to arouse in them a keen desire to reach personally verified conclusions upon all questions of general concernment to mankind, or of special significance for their own time. There is much truth in some remarks recently made in this connection by a college president:

Certain professors have been refused reelection lately, apparently because they set their students to thinking in ways objectionable to the trustees. It would be well if more teachers were dismissed because they fail to stimulate thinking of any kind. We can afford to forgive a college professor what we regard as the occasional error of his doctrine, especially as we may be wrong, provided he is a contagious center of intellectual enthusiasm. It is better for students to think about heresies than not to think at all; better for them to climb new trails, and stumble over error if need be, than to ride forever in upholstered ease in the overcrowded highway. It is a primary duty of a teacher to make a student take an honest account of his stock of ideas, throw out the dead matter, place revised price marks on what is left, and try to fill his empty shelves with new goods.

It is, however, possible and necessary that such intellectual awakening be brought about with patience, considerateness, and pedagogical wisdom.

There is one further consideration with regard to the classroom utterances of college and university teachers to which the committee thinks it important to call the attention of members of the profession, and of administrative authorities. Such utterances ought always to be considered privileged communications. Discussions in the classroom ought not to be supposed to be utterances for the public at large. They are often designed to provoke opposition or arouse debate. It has, unfortunately, sometimes happened in this country that sensational newspapers have quoted and garbled such remarks. As a matter of common law, it is clear that the utterances of an academic instructor are privileged, and may not be published, in whole or part, without his authorization. But our practice, unfortunately, still differs from that of foreign countries, and no effective check has in this country been put upon such unauthorized and often misleading publication. It is much to be desired that test cases should be made of any infractions of the rule.

In their extramural utterances, it is obvious that academic teachers are under a peculiar obligation to avoid hasty or unverified or exaggerated statements, and to refrain from intemperate or sensational modes of expression. But, subject to these restraints, it is not, in this committee's opinion, desirable that scholars should be debarred from giving expression to their judgments upon controversial questions, or that their freedom of speech, outside the university, should be limited to questions falling within their own specialties. It is clearly not proper that they should be prohibited from lending their active support to organized movements which they believe to be in the public interest. And, speaking broadly, it may be said in the words of a nonacademic body already once quoted in a publication of this Association, that "it is neither possible nor desirable to deprive a college professor of the political rights vouchsafed to every citizen."

It is, however, a question deserving of consideration by members of this Association, and by university officials, how far academic teachers, at least those dealing with political, economic, and social subjects, should be prominent in the management of our great party organizations, or should be candidates for state or national offices of a distinctly political character. It is manifestly desirable that such teachers have minds untrammeled by party loyalties, unexcited by party enthusiasms, and unbiased by personal political ambitions; and that universities should remain uninvolved in party antagonisms. On the other hand, it is equally manifest that the material available for the service of the state would be restricted in a highly undesirable way, if it were understood that no member of the academic profession should ever be called upon to assume the responsibilities of public office. This question may, in the committee's opinion, suitably be made a topic for special discussion at some future meeting of this Association, in order that a practical policy, which shall do justice to the two partially conflicting considerations that bear upon the matter, may be agreed upon.

It is, it will be seen, in no sense the contention of this committee that academic freedom implies that individual teachers should be exempt from all restraints as to the matter or manner of their utterances, either within or without the university. Such restraints as are necessary should in the main, your committee holds, be self-imposed, or enforced by the public opinion of the profession. But there may, undoubtedly, arise occasional cases in which the aberrations of individuals may require to be checked by definite disciplinary action. What this report chiefly maintains is that such action cannot with safety be taken by bodies not composed of members of the academic profession. Lay governing boards are competent to judge concerning charges of habitual neglect of assigned duties, on the part of individual teachers, and concerning charges of grave moral delinquency. But in matters of opinion, and of the utterance of opinion, such boards cannot intervene without destroying, to the extent of their intervention, the essential nature of a university—without converting it from a place dedicated to openness of mind, in which the conclusions expressed are the tested conclusions of trained scholars, into a place barred against the access of new light, and precommitted to the opinions or prejudices of men who have not been set apart or expressly trained for the scholar's duties. It is, in short, not the absolute freedom of utterance of the individual scholar, but the absolute freedom of thought, of inquiry, of discussion and of teaching, of the academic profession, that is asserted by this declaration of principles. It is conceivable that our profession may prove unworthy of its high calling, and unfit to exercise the responsibilities that belong to it. But it will scarcely be said as yet to have given evidence of such unfitness. And the existence of this Association, as it seems to your committee, must be construed as a pledge, not only that the profession will earnestly guard those liberties without which it cannot rightly render its distinctive and indispensable service to society, but also that it will with equal earnestness seek to maintain such standards of professional character, and of scientific integrity and competency, as shall make it a fit instrument for that service.

Edwin R. A. Seligman (Economics),
    Columbia University, *Chairman*

Charles E. Bennett (Latin),
    Cornell University

James Q. Dealey (Political Science),
    Brown University

Richard T. Ely (Economics),
    University of Wisconsin

Henry W. Farnam (Political Science),
    Yale University

Frank A. Fetter (Economics),
    Princeton University

Franklin H. Giddings (Sociology),
  Columbia University

Charles A. Kofoid (Zoology),
  University of California

Arthur O. Lovejoy (Philosophy),
  The Johns Hopkins University

Frederick W. Padelford (English),
  University of Washington

Roscoe Pound (Law),
  Harvard University

Howard C. Warren (Psychology),
  Princeton University

Ulysses G. Weatherly (Sociology),
  Indiana University

Excerpts from the 1940 *Statement of Principles on Academic Freedom and Tenure* with 1970 Interpretive Comments

The purpose of this statement is to promote public understanding and support of academic freedom and tenure and agreement upon procedures to ensure them in colleges and universities. Institutions of higher education are conducted for the common good and not to further the interest of either the individual teacher[1] or the institution as a whole. The common good depends upon the free search for truth and its free exposition.

Academic freedom is essential to these purposes and applies to both teaching and research. Freedom in research is fundamental to the advancement of truth. Academic free-

1. The word "teacher" as used in this document is understood to include the investigator who is attached to an academic institution without teaching duties.

dom in its teaching aspect is fundamental for the protection of the rights of the teacher in teaching and of the student to freedom in learning. It carries with it duties correlative with rights. **[1]**[2]

Tenure is a means to certain ends; specifically: (1) freedom of teaching and research and of extramural activities, and (2) a sufficient degree of economic security to make the profession attractive to men and women of ability. Freedom and economic security, hence, tenure, are indispensable to the success of an institution in fulfilling its obligations to its students and to society.

Academic Freedom

(a) Teachers are entitled to full freedom in research and in the publication of the results, subject to the adequate performance of their other academic duties; but research for pecuniary return should be based upon an understanding with the authorities of the institution.

(b) Teachers are entitled to freedom in the classroom in discussing their subject, but they should be careful not to introduce into their teaching controversial matter which has no relation to their subject.**[2]** Limitations of academic freedom because of religious or other aims of the institution should be clearly stated in writing at the time of the appointment.**[3]**

2. Boldface numbers in brackets refer to Interpretive Comments which follow.

(c) College and university teachers are citizens, members of a learned profession, and officers of an educational institution. When they speak or write as citizens, they should be free from institutional censorship or discipline, but their special position in the community imposes special obligations. As scholars and educational officers, they should remember that the public may judge their profession and their institution by their utterances. Hence they should at all times be accurate, should exercise appropriate restraint, should show respect for the opinions of others, and should make every effort to indicate that they are not speaking for the institution.[4]

1970 Interpretive Comments

Following extensive discussions on the 1940 *Statement of Principles on Academic Freedom and Tenure* with leading educational associations and with individual faculty members and administrators, a joint committee of the AAUP and the Association of American Colleges met during 1969 to reevaluate this key policy statement. On the basis of the comments received, and the discussions that ensued, the joint committee felt the preferable approach was to formulate interpretations of the *Statement* in terms of the experience gained in implementing and applying the *Statement* for over thirty years and of adapting it to current needs.

The committee submitted to the two associations for their consideration the following "Interpretive Comments." These interpretations were adopted by the Council of the American Association of University Professors in April

1970 and endorsed by the Fifty-sixth Annual Meeting as Association policy.

In the thirty years since their promulgation, the principles of the 1940 *Statement of Principles on Academic Freedom and Tenure* have undergone a substantial amount of refinement. This has evolved through a variety of processes, including customary acceptance, understandings mutually arrived at between institutions and professors or their representatives, investigations and reports by the American Association of University Professors, and formulations of statements by that association either alone or in conjunction with the Association of American Colleges. These comments represent the attempt of the two associations, as the original sponsors of the 1940 *Statement,* to formulate the most important of these refinements. Their incorporation here as Interpretive Comments is based upon the premise that the 1940 *Statement* is not a static code but a fundamental document designed to set a framework of norms to guide adaptations to changing times and circumstances.

Also, there have been relevant developments in the law itself reflecting a growing insistence by the courts on due process within the academic community which parallels the essential concepts of the 1940 *Statement;* particularly relevant is the identification by the Supreme Court of academic freedom as a right protected by the First Amendment. As the Supreme Court said in *Keyishian v. Board of Regents,* 385 U.S. 589 (1967), "Our Nation is deeply committed to safeguarding academic freedom, which is of transcendent value to all of us and not merely to the teachers concerned. That freedom is therefore a special concern of the First Amendment, which does not tolerate laws that cast a pall of orthodoxy over the classroom."

The numbers refer to the designated portion of the 1940 *Statement* on which interpretive comment is made.

[1] The Association of American Colleges and the American Association of University Professors have long recognized that membership in the academic profession carries with it special responsibilities. Both associations either separately or jointly have consistently affirmed these responsibilities in major policy statements, providing guidance to professors in their utterances as citizens, in the exercise of their responsibilities to the institution and to students, and in their conduct when resigning from their institution or when undertaking government-sponsored research. Of particular relevance is the *Statement on Professional Ethics,* adopted in 1966 as Association policy. (A revision, adopted in 1987, may be found in AAUP, *Policy Documents and Reports,* 9th ed. [Washington, D.C., 2001], 133–34.)

[2] The intent of this statement is not to discourage what is "controversial." Controversy is at the heart of the free academic inquiry which the entire statement is designed to foster. The passage serves to underscore the need for teachers to avoid persistently intruding material which has no relation to their subject.

[3] Most church-related institutions no longer need or

desire the departure from the principle of academic freedom implied in the 1940 *Statement,* and we do not now endorse such a departure.

[4] This paragraph is the subject of an interpretation adopted by the sponsors of the 1940 *Statement* immediately following its endorsement which reads as follows:

> If the administration of a college or university feels that a teacher has not observed the admonitions of paragraph (c) of the section on Academic Freedom and believes that the extramural utterances of the teacher have been such as to raise grave doubts concerning the teacher's fitness for his or her position, it may proceed to file charges under paragraph 4 of the section on Academic Tenure. In pressing such charges, the administration should remember that teachers are citizens and should be accorded the freedom of citizens. In such cases the administration must assume full responsibility, and the American Association of University Professors and the Association of American Colleges are free to make an investigation.

Paragraph (c) of the section on Academic Freedom in the 1940 *Statement* should also be interpreted in keeping with the 1964 "Committee A Statement on Extramural Utterances" (*Policy Documents and Reports,* 32), which states inter alia: "The controlling principle is that a faculty member's expression of opinion as a citizen cannot constitute grounds for dismissal unless it clearly demonstrates the faculty member's unfitness for his or her position. Extramural utterances rarely bear upon the faculty member's fitness for the position. Moreover, a final decision should take into account the faculty member's entire record as a teacher and scholar."

Paragraph 5 of the *Statement on Professional Ethics* also deals with the nature of the "special obligations" of the teacher. The paragraph reads as follows:

As members of their community, professors have the rights and obligations of other citizens. Professors measure the urgency of other obligations in the light of their responsibilities to their subject, to their students, to their profession, and to their institution. When they speak or act as private persons they avoid creating the impression of speaking or acting for their college or university. As citizens engaged in a profession that depends upon freedom for its health and integrity, professors have a particular obligation to promote conditions of free inquiry and to further public understanding of academic freedom.

Both the protection of academic freedom and the requirements of academic responsibility apply not only to the full-time probationary and the tenured teacher, but also to all others, such as part-time faculty and teaching assistants, who exercise teaching responsibilities.

Notes

Introduction

1. Michael Ferguson, *Creating Common Ground: Common Reading and the First Year of College,* Peer Review, Summer 2006, at 8, 8.

2. UNC General Alumni Association, *Summer Reading Program Panel Picks First Novel,* The Namesake, Jan. 28, 2006, https://alumni.unc.edu/article.aspx?SID=3533.

3. The committee ran paid advertisements in the *News & Observer* and in the *Daily Tar Heel* on June 27, 2003. The committee had also attacked the 2002 university assignment of Michael Sells's book *Approaching the Qur'an: The Early Revelations.* Kate Zernike, *Assigned Reading on Koran in Chapel Hill Raises Hackles,* N.Y. Times, Aug. 20, 2002, at A1. The university was sued for that assignment on the theory that it had violated students' rights to the free exercise of religion. The suit was ultimately dismissed. *Yacovelli v. Moeser,* 324 F. Supp. 2d 760 (M.D.N.C. 2004).

4. Jane Stancil, *Legislators Visit UNC-CH,* News & Observer, July 17, 2003, at B1; Eric Ferreri, *Legislators: UNC Book Choice Offensive, Dishonest,* Chapel Hill Herald, July 17, 2003, at 1. "Referencing last year's summer reading controversy over a book about Islam, [state senator Austin] Allran suggested that Carolina is fostering an anti-Christian environment." *Id.*

5. Eric Ferreri, *After Scrutiny, UNC Groups Discuss Book,* Chapel Hill Herald, Aug. 26, 2003, at 1.

6. *Id.*

7. *Report of the Committee of Inquiry on the Case of Professor Scott Nearing of the University of Pennsylvania,* 2 AAUP Bull. 7, 58 (1916). The AAUP committee of inquiry concluded that "at least a contributory cause of Dr. Nearing's removal was the opposition of certain persons outside the University to the views, upon questions within his own field of study, expressed by him in his extra-mural addresses. Removal or refusal of appointment, wholly or partly upon such a ground, without judicial inquiry by any committee of fellow-economists or other scholars, the committee can only regard as an infringement of academic freedom." *Id.* at 41.

8. "[Senator Ham] Horton said he didn't want academic leaders to misunderstand legislators' intent. 'I hope no one at the university thinks we're trying to throttle freedom of expression,' he said. 'We're just suggesting a different approach.'" Stancil, *supra* note 4.

9. *See also* Jane Stancil, *Lawmakers Bash Book Choice,* News & Observer, July 10, 2003, at B1 [hereinafter Stancil, *Lawmakers*]; Jane Stancil, *Students to Confront Moeser,* News & Observer, Aug. 15, 2003, at B1.

10. Consider that in 2003 a bill was introduced in Congress and passed by the House that required close scrutiny of federal funds supporting university centers focusing on foreign countries, on the ground that programs in Middle Eastern studies exhibited a systematic political bias. It was urged that the faculty in these programs were under the spell of the "post-colonial theory" of Edward Said and hence that they were overly critical of the United States and Israel. The proposed statute was designed to ensure that the activities of federally supported centers would

"reflect diverse perspectives and the full range of views on world regions . . . and international affairs." International Studies in Higher Education Act of 2003, H.R. 3077, 108th Cong. (passed by House, Oct. 21, 2003). Just as the Committee for a Better North Carolina maintained that it did not intend to cast a pall of orthodoxy over the classroom, but instead to dispel the uniform prejudice of a tendentious left-wing professoriat, so the proponents of the federal statute argued: "Naturally, it is right and proper that projects funded by Title VI are governed according to standards of free speech and academic freedom. Free speech, however, is not an entitlement to a government subsidy. And unless steps are taken to balance university faculties with members who both support and oppose American foreign policy, the very purpose of free speech and academic freedom will have been defeated." *International Programs in Higher Education and Questions of Bias: Hearing before the Subcomm. on Select Education of the Comm. on Education and the Workforce,* 108th Cong. 74 (2003) (written statement of Dr. Stanley Kurtz, Research Fellow, Hoover Institution, and Contributing Editor, National Review Online).

11. A recent bill proposed in Colorado to protect the so-called Academic Bill of Rights declares that "students have a right to expect that their academic freedom will not be infringed by instructors who create a hostile environment toward their political or religious beliefs." H.B. 04–1315, 64th Gen. Assem., 2d Reg. Sess. (Colo. 2004). The Colorado bill was withdrawn, but similar bills have been introduced in California, Florida, Georgia, Hawaii, Indiana, Kansas, Maine, Massachusetts, Maryland, New York, North Carolina, Ohio, Rhode Island, South Dakota, Tennessee, and Washington. None has passed, though several are still pending.

12. Although anecdotal allegations of abuse abound, in fact there is little systematic evidence to substantiate these charges. In 2005, the Pennsylvania legislature authorized an investigation into the condition of academic freedom in public institutions of higher education because it believed that students "should be protected from the imposition of ideological orthodoxy, and faculty members have the responsibility to not take advantage of their authority position to introduce inappropriate or irrelevant

subject matter outside their field of study." H.R. 177, 2005 Gen. Assem. (Pa.) (as amended by House, July 5, 2005). After holding nine days of hearings across the state over an eight-month period, the Select Committee on Academic Freedom in Higher Education reported that it had not identified any instance of a faculty member's use of his or her authority in that way. *Report of the Select Committee on Academic Freedom in Higher Education Pursuant to House Resolution 177* (Pa. 2006). The ranking minority member reported that the only example of bias given the committee was of a biology professor who had allegedly shown the film *Fahrenheit 9/11* to a class shortly before the 2004 election. Investigation revealed that the film was not shown on campus. *Id.* at 17.

We note that as this manuscript goes to press, the National Association of Scholars has launched the Argus Project to enlist volunteer "monitors" to report to it on whether the institution under surveillance "conducts politicized teaching" or "sustains slights to conservative students." *Big Argus Is Watching You,* Inside Higher Ed, July 30, 2008, http://www.insidehighered.com/news/2008/07/30/argus.

13. *E.g.,* Julia E. Johnsen, *Academic Freedom* (Reference Shelf Vol. 3, No. 6, 1925) (a series "presenting selected bibliography, briefs, and reprints . . . on both sides of the subject").

14. See, for example, the comments of Richard Rorty: "As Americans use the term, 'academic freedom' names some complicated local folkways that have developed in the course of the past century, largely as a result of battles fought by the American Association of University Professors. These customs and traditions insulate colleges and universities from politics and from public opinion. In particular, they insulate teachers from pressure from the public bodies or private boards who pay their wages." Richard Rorty, *Does Academic Freedom Have Philosophical Presuppositions?, in The Future of Academic Freedom* 21, 21 (Louis Menand ed., 1996).

15. Jennifer Jacobson, *The Clash over Middle East Studies: Critics Say the Programs Are Biased against U.S. Foreign Policy and Need a Review Board,* Chron. Higher Educ., Feb. 6, 2004, at A8.

16. Indeed, a legal scholar has even written, "If we are ever to

have a stable system of academic freedom, we must each take the definition of academic freedom we subscribe to and extend to other people whatever rights of academic freedom we claim for ourselves." Jennifer Bankier, *Academic Freedom and Reciprocity: Practicing What We Preach, in Academic Freedom and the Inclusive University* 136, 143 (Sharon Kahn & Dennis Pavlich eds., 2000).

17. In the controversy over *Nickel and Dimed,* for example, Austin Allran, a state senator who had criticized the University of North Carolina, was quoted as saying, "The university needs to cut back on its arrogance and start caring about the people who are paying the bills there." Stancil, *Lawmakers, supra* note 9.

18. For recent cases, see, for example, *Grutter v. Bollinger,* 539 U.S. 306 (2003), and *Regents of the University of California v. Bakke,* 438 U.S. 265 (1978).

19. On the distinction between constitutional and professional academic freedom, see Walter P. Metzger, *Profession and Constitution: Two Definitions of Academic Freedom in America,* 66 Texas L. Rev. 1265 (1988), and David M. Rabban, *Academic Freedom, in Encyclopedia of the American Constitution* 12 (Leonard W. Levy & Kenneth L. Karst eds., 1986).

20. *See* Matthew W. Finkin, *The Case for Tenure* (1996).

Chapter 1. The Historical Origins of the Concept of Academic Freedom

1. Leonard Levy, *Blasphemy* 7 (1993):

That the Athens of the fifth century B.C. could drive Socrates, Phidias, and Protagoras to their deaths and drive away Anaxagoras, Alcibiades, and Diagoras proved rather early in the history of the West that religion, when supported by the state, can be hostile to enlightenment and personal liberty. The record does not show that any of the victims reviled the deities. The cases tended to be as much political as religious in character. Treason against the gods was close to treason against the state, but Athens could accept a charge of impiety more easily than it could a political charge. Its targets of attack were mainly intellectual dissidents. Without exception, their cases raised fundamental issues of freedom of expression—literary, artistic, philosophical, religious, and political. Proof of a political charge against the state was harder to come by than proof of deviant religious opinion.

See also Robert Parker, *Athenian Religion* ch. 10 (1966) (on the trial of Socrates).

2. Louis Ginzberg, *Legends of the Bible* 441 (1992).

3. Indeed, the Inquisition's 1633 judgment of Galileo has been on trial ever since. The subject is explored in Maurice Finocchiaro, *Retrying Galileo, 1633–1992* (2005), Marco Biagioli, *Galileo, Courtier: The Practice of Science in the Culture of Absolutism* (1993), and Wade Rowland, *Galileo's Mistake* 265–66 (2001). No less a figure than Stephen Jay Gould has suggested that Galileo would have been better served—and science none the worse for it—had Galileo maintained Copernicanism as "a mathematical hypothesis rather than as empirical truth." Stephen Jay Gould, *The Hedgehog, the Fox, and the Magister's Pox* 88 (2003). Gould's suggestion regarding Galileo might be compared to his alarm at the idea that evolution should be taught as a "hypothesis." Stephen Jay Gould, *Rocks of Ages: Science and Religion in the Fullness of Life* (1999).

4. Galileo's prestige, diplomacy, and network of well-placed supporters—coupled with his timely recantation—saved him from a similar fate thirty-three years later. Galileo suffered only house arrest and the proscription of his work. A full account of Bruno's trial was published in Italian, Luigi Firpo, *Il processo di Giordane Bruno* (1993), but it has not been translated into English. Some good information is supplied in a review essay by Hilary Gatti, 3 Brit. J. Hist. Phil. 164 (1995), and in Michael White, *The Pope and the Heretic* (2002).

5. Hans Blumenberg, *The Genesis of the Copernican World* 372–73 (Robert Wallace trans., 1987); *id.* at 374 ("Bruno really was an *eretico obstinatissimo* [very obstinate heretic], as the *Avrisi di Roma* called him shortly before his *solennissime iustizia* [very solemn execution]."). Such was the pressure generated

by the Bruno case that, according to Carlo Ginzburg, it figured in the execution in late 1599 of the poor miller Domenico Scandella for his recidivist expressions of religious disbelief. Carlo Ginzburg, *The Cheese and the Worms: The Cosmos of a Sixteenth-Century Miller* 127–28 (John Tedeschi & Anne Tedeschi trans., 1980).

6. The dedication of 1588 has been translated into Italian and appears in Guido Calogero, *La professione di fede di Giordano Bruno,* 1 La Cultura 4 (1963). We wish to express our deep appreciation to Susan Mackenzie of Brussels for translating the quoted portion from that Italian edition into English. While that was being done we requested the medievalist Professor William Levitan to translate the original. Although these two translations are almost identical, we have used Professor Levitan's rendition of the original Latin *ad liberas disciplinas* to mean "freedom to teach."

7. Wade Rowland, *Galileo's Mistake* 116 (2001).

8. J. M. M. H. Thijssen, *Censure and Heresy at the University of Paris, 1200–1400,* at 114 (1998).

9. François Berriot, *Hétérodoxie religieuse et utopic politique dans les "erreus estranges" de Noël Journet* (1582), *in Spiritualités, Hétérodoxie et Imaginairs* 303, 303 (1994) (our translation).

10. Rodolphe Peter, *Noël Journet, Détracteur de l'Écriture sainte* (1582), *in Croyants et sceptiques au XVIe siècle* 147 (Marc Leinhard ed., 1981).

11. Carlo Ginzburg, *High and Low: The Theme of Forbidden Knowledge in the Sixteenth and Seventeenth Centuries,* 73 Past & Present 28, 30 (1976).

12. Neil Kenny, *The Uses of Curiosity in Early Modern France and Germany* 4 (2004): "Whereas from antiquity through the sixteenth century curiosity had most often—but not always—been a vice, especially from the seventeenth century onwards it was often morally neutral or positive. Curiosity was still commonly considered a vice, but now also often a healthy passion. The knowledge and behaviour produced by curiosity had previously been considered largely defective, but it was now considered either defective, morally neutral, or admirable."

13. Ginzburg, *supra* note 11, at 38, 41.

14. Immanuel Kant, *An Answer to the Question: "What is Enlightenment?," in Kant: Political Writings* 54, 54 (Hans Reiss ed., H. B. Nisbet trans., 1970).

15. J. Robert Oppenheimer, *The Relation of Research to the Liberal University, in Freedom and the University* 93, 95–96 (1950).

16. Marcia Colish, *Medieval Foundations of the Western Intellectual Tradition 400–1400*, at 325 (1997).

17. Daniel Headrick, *When Information Came of Age: Technologies of Knowledge in the Age of Reason and Revolution, 1700–1850*, at 9 (2000).

18. The intimate connection between commerce and science, between commerce and what we conceive of as knowledge, is explored by Harold Cook, who concludes of the late seventeenth and early eighteenth centuries that "countless people were involved in the production, accumulation, and exchange of the natural knowledge upon which commerce depended, and the high value they placed on accurate description of the created world—those 'matters of fact' that would be true in any circumstance—became a measuring stick according to which they could judge other forms of knowing. Valuing natural knowledge of such a kind suited activities based on exchanging goods rather than on seeking the Good, for deep in the roots of this kind of knowledge economy lay a moral economy weighted according to bodily pleasures and pains." Harold Cook, *Matters of Exchange* 41 (2007).

19. David Fellman, *Academic Freedom, in* 1 *Dictionary of the History of Ideas: Studies of Selected Pivotal Ideas* 9, 10 (Philip Weiner ed., 1973). Scientific investigation and commerce often went hand in hand. Witness the conjoined scientific and commercial activities of the members of the Lunar Society of Birmingham in the eighteenth century—the manufacturers Matthew Boulton, James Watt, and Josiah Wedgwood; the physician Erasmus Darwin; and the divine Joseph Priestley. Jennifer Uglo, *The Lunar Men* (2002).

20. Anthony Grafton, *Defenders of the Text: The Tradition of Scholarship in an Age of Science, 1450–1800* ch. 8 (1991).

21. *Id.* at 205.

22. The account of the Wolff case is taken from Otfried Nip-

pold, *Introduction* to Christian Wolff, *Jus gentium methodo scientifica pertractatum,* at xiii (Joseph Drake trans., 1934), and Wolfgang Dreschler, *Christian Wolff (1679–1754): A Biographical Essay, in Christian Wolff and Law & Economics* 1 (Jürgen Backhaus ed., 1998).

23. Drechsler, *supra* note 22, at 114.

24. Michael Albrecht, *Einleitung, in* Christian Wolff, *Oratio de Sinarum philosophia practica: Rede über die praktische Philosophie der Chinesen,* at ix, liii (Michael Albrecht ed., 1985) (our translation).

25. Hans Thieme, *Die Geschichtlichen Voraussetzungen für Artikel 5,3 des Grundgesetzes der Bundesrepublik Deutschland, in Die Freiheit der Künste und Wissenschaften* 7, 16 (1967) (our translation).

26. *Id.*

27. Thijssen, *supra* note 8, at 91. Marcia Colish connects the want of academic freedom in Muslim institutions of the Middle Ages to the absence of institutional autonomy: "Starting in the eleventh century, rulers and wealthy patrons making charitable donations established *madrasas,* centers for advanced study of the religious sciences whose teachers gave formal accreditation to students demonstrating mastery of these subjects. Whether the patrons of *madrasas* were public or private, the legal structure of their foundation charters gave them control over the theological and legal interpretations taught there and over academic personnel. These schools and their faculties had no collective authority, in part because Muslim law lacked the concept of the legal corporation. Academic freedom was thus non-existent. Students were expected to accept the views of their teachers and teachers were required to profess the views of the founders." Colish, *supra* note 16, at 131.

28. Thijssen, *supra* note 8, at 115.

29. *Id.* at 89.

30. Heiko Oberman, *Luther: Man Between God and the Devil* 22 (1989).

31. *Id.* at 23.

32. On the church's concern over publication in a language comprehensible to common people, see William Eamon, *From*

the Secrets of Nature to Public Knowledge, in Reappraisals of the Scientific Revolution 333 (David Lindberg & Robert Westman eds., 1990). We omit here reference to the extensive history of book and pamphlet publication, of efforts at licensing and control, and of resistance by authors and printers, smugglers and sellers.

33. Richard Hofstadter & Walter P. Metzger, *The Development of Academic Freedom in the United States* 373 (1955).

34. David Hollinger, *The Knower and the Artificer, in Modernist Impulses in the Human Sciences* 26, 33 (Dorothy Ross ed., 1994).

35. It has been argued that this provision spoke more to the independence of institutions than to the independence of the faculties within them. This account and what follows is taken from Thieme, *supra* note 25, at 19.

36. Thieme, *supra* note 25, at 20 (our translation).

37. Hermann von Helmholtz, *Über die akademische Freiheit der deutschen Universitäten, reprinted in Idee und Wirklichkeit Einer Universität* 391, 399 (Wilhelm Weischedel ed., 1960) (our translation).

38. Abraham Flexner, *Universities: American, English, German* 317–18 (1930).

39. Christopher Jencks & David Riesman, *The Academic Revolution* 160 (1967).

40. Walter P. Metzger, *Academic Tenure in America: A Historical Essay, in Faculty Tenure: A Report and Recommendations by the Commission on Academic Tenure in Higher Education* 93, 115 (1973).

41. Alton Parker, *The Rights of Donors,* 23 Educ. Rev. 16, 21 (1902).

42. Hofstadter & Metzger, *supra* note 33, at 331.

43. Andrew Dickson White, *A History of the Warfare of Science with Theology in Christendom* (1896).

44. Letter from Andrew Dickson White to Daniel Coit Gilman (July 24, 1878), *reprinted in* 2 *American Higher Education: A Documentary History* 848, 848 (Richard Hofstadter & Wilson Smith eds., 1967).

45. The board of regents declared: "Whatever may be the limitations which trammel inquiry elsewhere, we believe that the great state University of Wisconsin should ever encourage that controversial and fearless sifting and winnowing by which alone the truth can be found." *See generally Academic Freedom on Trial: 100 Years of Sifting and Winnowing at the University of Wisconsin–Madison* 1 (W. Lee Hansen ed., 1998).

Chapter 2. The 1915 *Declaration* and the American Concept of Academic Freedom

1. Richard Hofstadter & Walter P. Metzger, *The Development of Academic Freedom in the United States* 388–89 (1955). The influences of this worry are manifest in early statements of American academic freedom. As the dean of Columbia Law School Harlan Fiske Stone proclaimed, "Especially do I hold to the opinion that the university professor should voluntarily renounce the role of the propagandist and the agitator. The university stands for scientific truth. Its attitude, if it would preserve its influence, must never be that of the partisan, but rather that of the judicially minded. The university professor in acting such a part inevitably subjects the university as well as himself to partisan attack in a controversy in which it can with propriety take no part and to which it is powerless to offer a defense." Harlan F. Stone, *University Influence,* 20 Colum. U. Q. 330, 338 (1918). The original academic-freedom policy of the University of California, promulgated by President Robert Gordon Sproul in 1934, advanced a vision of professional vocation that was deeply influenced by the idea of a "dispassionate" scholarship that, when it considered "political, social or sectarian movements," merely "dissected and examined" and left "the conclusion . . . with no tipping of the scales, to the logic of the facts." Richard C. Atkinson, *Academic Freedom and the Research University,* http://www.ucop.edu/ucophome/coordrev/policy/Academic_Freedom_Paper.pdf, *reprinted in* 148 Proc. Am. Phil. Soc'y 195, 196–97 (2004). The University of California recently revised its academic-freedom policy explicitly to reject this vision of the professoriat:

The original language of APM-010, which was drafted in 1934, associated academic freedom with scholarship that gave "play to intellect rather than to passion." . . . The revised version of APM-010 holds that academic freedom depends upon the quality of scholarship, which is to be assessed by the content of scholarship, not by the motivations that led to its production. The revision of APM-010 therefore does not distinguish between "interested" and "disinterested" scholarship; it differentiates instead between competent and incompetent scholarship. Although competent scholarship requires an open mind, this does not mean that faculty are unprofessional if they reach definite conclusions. It means rather that faculty must always stand ready to revise their conclusions in the light of new evidence or further discussion. Although competent scholarship requires the exercise of reason, this does not mean that faculty are unprofessional if they are committed to a definite point of view. It means rather that faculty must form their point of view by applying professional standards of inquiry rather than by succumbing to external and illegitimate incentives such as monetary gain or political coercion. Competent scholarship can and frequently does communicate salient viewpoints about important and controversial questions.

University of California Academic Personnel Manual APM-010, *available at* http://www.ucop.edu/acadadv/acadpers/apm/apm-010.pdf; *see* Robert C. Post, *Academic Freedom and the "Intifada Curriculum,"* Academe, May–June 2003, at 16, 19 ("There is no academic norm that prohibits scholarship from communicating definite viewpoints about important and controversial questions, like democracy, human rights, or the welfare state. Faculty must be free to communicate these viewpoints in their pedagogy. Political passion is in fact the engine that drives some of the best scholarship and teaching at the University of California, and this is particularly true in the humanities and social sciences.").

2. Hofstadter & Metzger, *supra* note 1, at 403.

3. On the authorship of the 1915 *Declaration,* see Walter P. Metzger, *The 1940 Statement of Principles on Academic Freedom and Tenure,* 53 Law & Contemp. Probs. 3, 12–13 (1990),

reprinted in Freedom and Tenure in the Academy 3, 12–13 (William Van Alstyne ed., 1993).

4. Orrin Leslie Elliott, *Stanford University: The First Twenty-Five Years* 341 (1937). Eight days later, Mrs. Stanford wrote Jordan again: "There is a very deep and bitter feeling of indignation throughout the community . . . that Stanford University is lending itself to partisanism and even to dangerous socialism. . . . Professor Ross cannot be trusted, and he should go. . . . He is a dangerous man. Dear Dr. Jordan, I am very much in earnest in this matter, and I have just reasons for feeling so." *Id.* at 343–44. For a discussion of the case, see Mary O. Furner, *Advocacy & Objectivity: A Crisis in the Professionalization of American Social Science, 1865–1905,* at 229–59 (1975), Thomas L. Haskell, *Justifying the Rights of Academic Freedom in the Era of "Power/Knowledge," in The Future of Academic Freedom,* 43, 48–53 (Louis Menand ed., 1996), and Hofstadter & Metzger, *supra* note 1, at 436–45.

5. Editorial, *Academic Freedom,* N.Y. Times, June 20, 1915, at 14.

6. *Report of the Committee of Inquiry on the Case of Professor Scott Nearing of the University of Pennsylvania,* 2 AAUP Bull. 7, 10 (1916). Several months later the board offered a somewhat fuller explanation. *Id.* at 25–28.

7. Editorial, *The Philadelphia Martyr,* N.Y. Times, Oct. 10, 1915, at 29. "The professors and assistant professors," the *Times* sniffed, "are the chartered libertines of speech." *Id.* Responding to the public outcry over the termination of Scott Nearing, Wharton trustee J. Levering Jones remarked that "the University of Pennsylvania is not a public institution. It is only quasi-public. We are answerable only to our own sense of duty and responsibility. No one has the right to question us." Philadelphia Public Ledger, June 19, 1915. The premise of uncontestable control over employees echoes the notorious retort of George Baer, a spokesman for the anthracite coal industry, to public criticism of the anthracite coal companies' refusal to bargain with its miners: "The rights and interests of the laboring men will be protected and cared for . . . by the Christian men to whom God in his infinite wisdom has given control of the property interests of this country." Witt Bowden, *The Industrial History of the United States*

890 (1930). On the persistence in contemporary employment law of the attitude expressed by Jones and Baer, see Clyde Summers, *Employment at Will in the United States: The Divine Right of Employers,* 3 U. Pa. J. Lab. & Emp. L. 65 (2000).

8. *Payne v. Western & Atl. R.R.,* 81 Tenn. 507, 518–20 (1884).

9. Charles W. Eliot, *Academic Freedom,* Science, July 5, 1907, at 1, 3. Eliot noted that university boards could "exclude from the teachings of the university unpopular or dangerous subjects. In some states they even treat professors' positions as common political spoils; and all too frequently, both in state and endowed institutions, they fail to treat members of the teaching staff with that high consideration to which their functions entitle them." *Id.*

10. Evans Clark, *Business Men in Control of American Colleges,* N.Y. Times Mag., June 10, 1917, at 64.

11. *Id.*

12. *Academic Freedom, supra* note 5. For similar views, see Editorial, *Academic Freedom,* N.Y. Times, June 7, 1901, at 8, asserting that "the freedom of a man who spends his money for education to elect the sort of education for which he will spend it is, on the face of it, as well established a right as any that the educators can lay claim to," and Editorial, *Academic Freedom,* N.Y. Times, Mar. 4, 1903, at 8, questioning "the assumption that the teacher has a certain inherent right to be maintained at the cost of some one else without consulting any but his own judgment as to what or how he will teach" and asserting that "very few of us can successfully insist upon keeping our independence unimpaired and being paid for it."

13. John Dewey, Letter to the Editor, *Professorial Freedom,* N.Y. Times, Oct. 22, 1915, at 10.

14. Arthur O. Lovejoy, *Academic Freedom, in Encyclopedia of the Social Sciences* 384, 384 (Edwin R. A. Seligman & Alvin Johnson eds., 1930).

15. "The dispute between the upstart profession and entrenched regental authority . . . was seen, correctly, as a confrontation over the status of the faculty within the institution" of the university. Matthew W. Finkin, *Intramural Speech, Academic Freedom, and the First Amendment,* 66 Tex. L. Rev. 1323, 1335 (1988).

16. John Dewey had articulated the basis of this argument as

early as 1902: "It is necessary to make a distinction between the university proper and those teaching bodies, called by whatever name, whose primary business is to inculcate a fixed set of ideas and facts. The former aims to discover and communicate truth and to make its recipients better judges of truth and more effective in applying it to the affairs of life. The latter have as their aim the perpetuation of a certain way of looking at things current among a given body of persons. Their purpose is to disciple rather than to discipline—not indeed at the expense of truth, but in such a way as to conserve what is already regarded as truth by some considerable body of persons." John Dewey, *Academic Freedom,* 23 Educ. Rev. 1, 1 (1902). Dewey conceptualized the argument as resting on a distinction between an "obligation in behalf of all the truth to society at large" and an obligation "of a part of truth to a part of society." *Id.* at 2.

17. Lovejoy, *supra* note 14, at 384–85.

18. As Lovejoy would later put it: "A state may, in short, have a university or do without. But it cannot have one, in the usual and proper sense, if it excludes . . . the method of free inquiry and free expression, which is necessary to the functioning of this type of social institution." *Id.* at 385.

19. In his letter to the *New York Times* protesting its support of the University of Pennsylvania's firing of Nearing, Dewey objected: "You apparently take the ground that a modern university is a personally conducted institution like a factory, and that if for any reason the utterances of any teacher, within or without the university walls, are objectionable to the Trustees, there is nothing more to be said. This view virtually makes the Trustees owners of a private undertaking. . . . A discussion by The Times of whether modern universities should be conceived as privately owned and managed institutions, or as essentially public institutions, with responsibilities to the public, would be welcome." Dewey left no doubt that in his view "the modern university is in every respect, save its legal management, a public institution with public responsibilities." Dewey, *supra* note 13.

20. For a discussion, see Haskell, *supra* note 4, at 63–83, and David M. Rabban, *Can Academic Freedom Survive Postmodernism?,* 86 Calif. L. Rev. 1377 (1998).

21. On the interrelationship between professional standards of inquiry and the production of knowledge, see Haskell, *supra* note 4, at 63–64. On the relationship between scientific methodology and claims of academic freedom, see Hofstadter & Metzger, *supra* note 1, at 363–66.

22. "Aber es besteht kein Hindernis, ergend welche *wissen-schaftiche* Streitfrage *wissenschaftich* zu diskutieren." Hermann von Helmholtz, *Über die akademische Freiheit der deutschen Universitäten, reprinted in Idee und Wirklichkeit Einer Universität* 391, 399 (Wilhelm Weischedel ed., 1960). Importantly, the italics are in the original.

23. Lovejoy accurately caught the tension between individual freedom and professional obligations when he defined academic freedom as "the freedom of the teacher or research worker in higher institutions of learning to investigate and discuss the problems of his science and to express his conclusions, whether through publication or in the instruction of students, without interference from political or ecclesiastical authority, or from the administrative officials of the institution in which he is employed, *unless* his methods are found by qualified bodies of his own profession to be clearly incompetent or contrary to professional ethics." Lovejoy, *supra* note 14, at 384 (emphasis added).

24. What "sets academic freedom apart as a distinct freedom is its vocational claim of special and limited accountability in respect to all academically related pursuits of the teacher-scholar: an accountability not to any institutional or societal standard of economic benefit, acceptable interest, right thinking, or socially constructive theory, but solely to a fiduciary standard of professional integrity. . . . The maintenance of academic freedom contemplates an accountability in respect to academic investigations and utterances solely in respect of their professional integrity, a matter usually determined by reference to professional ethical standards of truthful disclosure and reasonable care." William Van Alstyne, *The Specific Theory of Academic Freedom and the General Issue of Civil Liberty, in The Concept of Academic Freedom* 59, 71 (Edmund Pincoffs ed., 1972).

25. Hence the conclusion of Thomas Haskell: "Historically speaking, the heart and soul of academic freedom lie not in free

speech but in professional autonomy and collegial self-governance. Academic freedom came into being as a defense of the disciplinary community (or, more exactly, the university conceived as an ensemble of such communities)." Haskell, *supra* note 4, at 54. There is of course an ambiguity at the heart of the notion of a single "academic profession" because in practice the profession always splinters into distinct disciplinary communities. This ambiguity is reflected in the persisting tension between the centrifugal force of departmental self-governance and the centripetal force of unified faculty self-governance, frequently in the form of a faculty senate.

26. The 1915 *Declaration* declares: "It is . . . inadmissible that the power of determining when departures from the requirements of the scientific spirit and method have occurred, should be vested in bodies not composed of members of the academic profession. Such bodies necessarily lack full competency to judge of those requirements; their intervention can never be exempt from the suspicion that it is dictated by other motives than zeal for the integrity of science. . . . It follows that university teachers must be prepared to assume this responsibility for themselves."

27. *McIntyre v. Ohio Elections Comm'n,* 514 U.S. 334, 342 (1995).

28. For a discussion, see Frederick Schauer, *Free Speech: A Philosophical Enquiry* 15–34 (1982).

29. *See* Robert Post, *Reconciling Theory and Doctrine in First Amendment Jurisprudence,* 88 Calif. L. Rev. 2355, 2363–66 (2000).

30. *See* Bernard Williams, *Truth & Truthfulness: An Essay in Genealogy* 213–19 (2002).

31. On the contemporary danger of such a reformulation, see Edward Shils, *Do We Still Need Academic Freedom,* 62 Am. Scholar 187, 188 (1993) ("Academic freedom . . . is no longer thought [to have] any close relationship to the search for or the affirmation of truths discovered by study and reflection. It has become part of the more general right of the freedom of expression. Expression is not confined to the expression of reasoned and logically and empirically supported statements; it now pretty much

extends to the expression of any desire, any sentiment, any impulse.").

32. Alexander Meiklejohn, *Political Freedom: The Constitutional Powers of the People* 27 (1960). *See* Laurence Tribe, *American Constitutional Law* 940–41 (2d ed. 1988) ("The presumption of the equality of ideas is a corollary of the basic requirement that the government may not aim at the communicative impact of expressive conduct.").

33. Post, *supra* note 29; Robert Post, *Equality and Autonomy in First Amendment Jurisprudence,* 95 Mich. L. Rev. 1517 (1997).

34. It might be said that in a democracy all private organizations ought to respect free and critical inquiry to the maximum extent compatible with the achievement of organizational objectives. *See* Robert Post, *Between Management and Governance: The History and Theory of the Public Forum,* 34 UCLA L. Rev. 1713 (1987). But on this account the objectives of higher education must be specified. If these objectives are said to include the production of knowledge, academic freedom will assume roughly the same contours as those advanced in the 1915 *Declaration.* But if, as is sometimes maintained, these objectives are instead said to include the exemplification of the democratic value of free and critical inquiry, academic freedom would appear to be rendered quite vulnerable. It does not take a deep social theorist to see that if universities claim to be contributing nothing more to the public good than embodying freedoms that all in a democratic society ought theoretically to enjoy, they would rapidly attract public resentment and jealousy rather than support. It would be neither effective nor persuasive for scholars to demand the special privileges of academic freedom on the ground that they happen to be lucky enough to be employed by institutions that exemplify freedoms that all ought in the abstract to possess. Members of a public willing to repress themselves could hardly be above the temptation to inflict similar repression on scholars who claim no function beyond shining forth the virtues of unregulated freedom, if for no other reason than to remove such painful symbols of what members of the public have themselves lost. Reduced to so fragile a state, academic freedom could scarcely offer the protections that faculty require.

35. Walter Metzger, *The First Investigation,* 47 AAUP Bull. 206 (1961).

36. *Report of Committee A on Academic Freedom and Tenure,* 4 AAUP Bull. 16, 20 (1918).

37. *Id.* at 18; *see also* Daniel Pollitt & Jordan Kurland, *Entering the Academic Freedom Arena Running: The AAUP's First Year,* Academe, July–Aug. 1998, at 45.

38. John Henry Wigmore, *Report of the President,* 2 AAUP Bull. 16 (1916).

39. The participants represented the American Assembly of University Women, the AAUP, the Association of American Colleges (AAC) (now the Association of American Colleges and Universities), the Association of American Universities, the Association of Governing Boards of Universities and Colleges, the Association of Land Grant Colleges, the Association of Urban Universities, the National Association of State Universities, and the American Council of Education. It proceeded on the basis of AAC drafts of 1922 and 1923.

40. William McGuffrey Hepburn, *Academic Freedom and Tenure,* 23 AAUP Bull. 642, 649 (1937).

41. Metzger, *supra* note 3.

42. *Id.* It is doubtful that representatives of research universities would have been so solicitous of the sensibilities of immature youth or of church-related institutions.

43. A review of institutional policies undertaken in 1953 referred to the 1940 *Statement* as "too well known" to require reiteration. Charles Dennison, *Faculty Rights and Obligations in Eight Independent Liberal Arts Colleges* 4 (1955).

44. *Report of Committee A for 1947,* 34 AAUP Bull. 110, 118 (1948).

45. Robert Lincoln Kelley, executive director of the AAC from 1917 to 1937, has explained: "It has been unanimously agreed that the American Association of University Professors should take the initiative in receiving and considering complaints, that it should have power to dismiss complaints after preliminary examinations, that those complaints which seemed to require fuller examination should be referred through the office of the Association of American Colleges to that Association's committee, and

that joint conferences should be held, if deemed necessary, before a judicial investigation should be undertaken by the American Association of University Professors. . . . From the time it [the AAUP] follows clues to the time it places colleges on the black list, it is responsible for the conduct of the cases." Robert Lincoln Kelly, *The American College and the Social Order* 124 (1940). The process of consultation, if it ever was implemented, fell into disuse.

46. On the process of policy formulation, see Ralph S. Brown Jr. & Matthew Finkin, *The Usefulness of AAUP Policy Statements,* 59 Educ. Rec. 30 (1978). For examples of Committee A policies, see *Committee A Statement on Extramural Utterances* (1964) (approved by Committee A), *reprinted in AAUP Policy Documents and Reports* 32 (10th ed. 2006), and *Statement on Professors and Political Activity* (1969) (amended in 1990) (approved by Committee A, adopted by the association's governing board, endorsed by its annual meeting and endorsed by the AAC), *reprinted in AAUP Policy Documents and Reports, supra,* at 33.

47. The AAUP's role as a mediator was studied by James Belasco, *The American Association of University Professors: A Private Dispute Settlement Agency,* 18 Ind. & Lab. Rel. Rev. 535 (1965).

48. The report, bearing the authorization of Committee A, is that body's document; very rarely, a member of an investigating committee will remove himself or herself as a signatory when he or she cannot agree with the parent body's position. Equally rarely, a member of Committee A may publicly dissent from the majority's view.

49. The history is explored by Jonathan Knight, *The AAUP's Censure List,* Academe, Jan.–Feb. 2003, at 44. From 1930, when a predecessor but weaker list of admonishment was published, to 2002, a total of 183 administrations were censured, some more than once.

50. The AAUP publishes an annual report about developments in negotiations with censured administrations.

51. *Browzin v. Catholic Univ.,* 527 F.2d 843, 848 n.8 (D.C. Cir. 1975) (observing as well that the AAUP's investigative reports "are noted for their thoroughness and scrupulous care"). In 1936,

the chairman of Committee A ruminated on the suggestion that a joint body of AAUP and administrative representatives serve as a "board of arbitration" to which, by agreement with colleges and universities, all deadlocked cases of faculty rights would be referred for final and binding decision. "It would be interesting," he observed, "to see how many institutions would be willing to subscribe to such an agreement." *Report of Committee A for 1936*, 23 AAUP Bull. 103, 106 (1937). The suggestion has gone no further.

52. In 1968, the student editors of the *Harvard Law Review* criticized the AAUP for missing "an opportunity to further the development of a consistent law of academic freedom by not utilizing its prior investigation decisions as precedents in later proceedings; instead, each report purports to be a direct, de novo application of the basic principles of the 1940 Statement to the facts of the instant dispute. To some extent this practice can be defended, for the willingness of all parties to accept an AAUP decision would be reduced if past reports rigidly were treated as stare decisis and consequently the hearing of the present dispute would seem perfunctory. But this danger would not be present if previous decisions were given recognition only in accordance with the cogency of their reasoning." *Developments in the Law: Academic Freedom*, 81 Harv. L. Rev. 1045, 1107 (1968) (citation omitted). In recent years, however, prior reports have been used much more explicitly as precedents. *See, e.g., Academic Freedom and Tenure: City University of New York*, Academe, Nov.–Dec. 2004, at 43; *Academic Freedom and Tenure: Philander Smith College (Arkansas)*, Academe, Jan.–Feb. 2004, at 57; *Academic Freedom and Tenure: University of Southern California*, Academe, Nov.–Dec. 1995, at 40; Special Report, *Hurricane Katrina and New Orleans Universities*, Academe, May–June 2007, at 59. The complete library of case investigations is now available on CD-ROM.

Chapter 3. Freedom of Research and Publication

1. The predecessor 1925 conference statement (see chapter 2, text accompanying notes 39–40) had provided: "A university or

college may not place any restraint upon the teacher's freedom in investigation, unless restriction upon the amount of time devoted to it becomes necessary in order to prevent undue interference with teaching duties." 18 AAUP Bull. 327 (1932).

2. Walter Metzger, *Academic Freedom and Scientific Freedom,* 107 Daedalus 93, 103 (1978).

3. Edward Shils, *Do We Still Need Academic Freedom,* 62 Am. Scholar 187, 194 (1993).

4. Joan W. Scott, *Academic Freedom as an Ethical Practice, in The Future of Academic Freedom* 163, 175 (Louis Menand ed., 1996).

5. Alexander Meiklejohn, *Political Freedom: The Constitutional Powers of the People* 27 (1960).

6. David Hollinger, *Cosmopolitanism and Solidarity: Studies in Ethnoracial, Religious, and Professional Affiliation in the United States* 79 (2006).

7. Louis Menand, *The Limits of Academic Freedom, in The Future of Academic Freedom, supra* note 4, at 3, 10.

8. Shils, *supra* note 3, at 203.

9. As Judith Jarvis Thomson has observed in the context of the role of collegial bodies in considering the appointment of faculty who challenge a discipline's prevailing models or methodologies: "While the new has the burden of proof, and the proof required is proof to the assessor, the assessor must exercise due care and must make his or her assessment on scholarly grounds, without excessive love for his or her own commitments. But having carried out that duty is compatible with having reached the wrong assessment." Judith Jarvis Thomson, *Ideology in Faculty Selection, in Freedom and Tenure in the Academy* 155, 163 (William Van Alstyne ed., 1993).

10. Thomas Kuhn, *The Structure of Scientific Revolutions* (2d ed. 1970). As Bernard Williams writes: "The orderly management of scientific inquiry implies that the vast majority of suggestions which an uninformed person might mistake for a contribution to science will, quite properly, not be taken seriously and will not find their way to discussion or publication. Very rarely the cranky view turns out to be right, and then the scientists who ignored it are attacked for dogmatism and prejudice. But, they can

rightly reply, there was no way of telling in advance that this particular cranky idea was to be taken seriously; the only alternative to their practice of prejudice would be to take seriously all such suggestions, and science would grind to a halt." Bernard Williams, *Truth and Truthfulness: An Essay in Genealogy* 217 (2002).

11. The interdependence of norms and social cohesion is a general phenomenon, plainly visible in the larger legal system. *See, e.g.,* Neil S. Siegel, *The Virtue of Judicial Statesmanship,* 86 Tex. L. Rev. 959 (2008).

12. *E.g.,* Drummond Rennie, *Thyroid Storm,* 277 JAMA 1238 (1997). *See generally Statement on Corporate Finding of Academic Research, reprinted in AAUP Policy Documents and Reports* 130 (10th ed. 2006). Conditions placed by outside funders on faculty research, especially if enforced by a university, may be inconsistent with freedom of research and publication. *See generally* Derek Bok, *Universities in the Marketplace* (2003); David L. Kirp, *Shakespeare, Einstein, and the Bottom Line: The Marketing of Higher Education* (2003); Jennifer Washburn, *University Inc.: The Corporate Corruption of American Higher Education* (2005). Institutional restrictions on faculty access to funding can also be in tension with freedom of research. In 1992, Committee A's opinion was sought regarding a university's refusal, on the ground of a foundation's sponsorship of research promoting theories of racial inferiority, to allow a faculty member to receive research funding from that foundation. Allowing the funds would allegedly compromise the institution's commitment to racial diversity. Committee A noted that although access to funds could be denied on administrative, nonideological grounds, or on the ground that grant conditions would limit academic freedom by preventing or curtailing the dissemination of the results, disapproval of the grantor's views was not an acceptable ground of regulation. "Denying a faculty member the opportunity to receive requisite funding improperly curtails the researcher's academic freedom no less than if the university took direct steps to halt research that it considered unpalatable. . . . The university should not assume responsibility for the views or attitudes of the funding agency, just as it is not expected to endorse the content of the researcher's work." The Committee noted as well that "an institution which

seeks to distinguish between and among different kinds of offensive corporate behavior presumes that it is competent to distinguish impermissible corporate wrongdoing from wrongful behavior that is acceptable. A university which starts down this path will find it difficult to resist demands that research bans should be imposed on other funding agencies that are seen as reckless or supportive of repellent programs." *An Issue of Academic Freedom in Refusing Outside Funding for Faculty Research,* Academe, Sept.–Oct. 1992, at 49. Committee A reiterated this position a decade later in response to reports that some universities had banned research sponsored by tobacco companies. *Academic Freedom and Rejection of Research Funds from Tobacco Corporations,* Academe, Sept.–Oct. 2003, at 83. To the AAUP it was irrelevant that the prohibition might have the support of an institution's faculty; no academic ground had been adduced that would justify the proposed prohibition.

13. *See generally* Robert Rosenbaum, *Federal Restrictions on Research: Academic Freedom and National Security,* Academe, Sept.–Oct. 1982, at 18a. The AAUP Special Committee on Academic Freedom and National Security in a Time of Crisis recently admonished:

It has become something of a commonplace to assume that security and freedom exist in an inherent and therefore ineluctable tension. This report questions that assumption. The free exchange of scientific data—for example, a component of a deadly toxin—may well help to equip a terrorist group with a means of mass destruction. But that same openness may better equip researchers to produce the means of preempting or neutralizing that very threat. Secrecy can impede the pace of scientific discovery for good as well as for ill. We are not alone in observing that freedom is often a critical component of security; it is not invariably inimical to it. The recent experience of the People's Republic of China, whose suppression of the full extent of the outbreak of SARS (severe acute respiratory syndrome) seriously exacerbated a threat to world health, with devastating human and economic consequences, stands as a caution to the assumption that secrecy always abets security.

Nevertheless, there may be points where some of our freedoms will have to yield to the manifest imperatives of security. What we should not accept is that we must yield those freedoms whenever the alarm of security is sounded. Given the extensive historical record of governmental overreaching and abuse in the name of security, we are right to be skeptical. Even at the height of the Cold War, when we faced the prospect of nuclear annihilation, the government did not institute security measures as far reaching as some now proposed. In other words, we are historically justified in insisting on a stringent standard of care. In the face of hateful foes who would destroy our institutions, we are right to remind the government and the public, as Committee A did in 1943, that an avowed object of our defense is the maintenance of these institutions, of which intellectual—and so academic—freedom is an inextricable part.

Academic Freedom and National Security in a Time of Crisis, Academe, Nov.–Dec. 2003, at 34, 37 (2003) (citations omitted).

14. *Academic Freedom at the University of Missouri,* 16 AAUP Bull. 143, 145 (1930).

15. The committee included the chairman, A. J. Carlson (University of Chicago), one of the nation's leading scientists (and later an AAUP president and one of the negotiators of the 1940 *Statement*); Louis L. Thurstone (University of Chicago), the founder of both the Psychometric Society and the journal *Psychometrika;* and Percy Bordwell (University of Iowa), a professor and then acting dean of the University of Iowa College of Law.

16. Lawrence Nelson, *Rumors of Indiscretion* (2003).

17. *Academic Freedom at the University of Missouri,* supra note 14, at 164–65.

18. *Id.* at 146.

19. *Id.* at 167.

20. *Id.* at 148–50. In its conclusion the committee acknowledged that DeGraff and Meyer had failed to take enough care to avoid offense. "The University Administration has the right to expect that when an instructor's teaching and research directly touches traditional taboos, as much care as possible be taken by

the instructor to minimize the chances for misunderstanding and uninformed criticism of the University, and consequent embarrassment of the Administration." *Id.* at 161. But the committee was nevertheless clear that notwithstanding this failure, the University should have defended DeGraff and Meyer from the resulting public outrage. "But since conflict between science and traditional taboos is inevitable and perennial, instructors in the University and citizens in general have the right to expect from the University Administration clear and courageous leadership in defense of the freedom of teaching and research, in addition to fairness and truth in explaining the criticized work to the public. President Brooks and the Board failed entirely in this duty on the questionnaire issue." *Id.* at 162.

21. *Id.* at 147.

22. *Id.* at 159.

23. *Id.* at 154, 175.

24. A Sedalia pastor saw the questionnaire as inspired by "Soviet Russia," as a "studied effort to undermine four of our basic cornerstones—the home, the school, the church and the state." Nelson, *supra* note 16, at 120.

25. *Id.* at 238.

26. If this lesson seems distant and anodyne, consider that in the spring of 2002, Francis Dane, a professor of psychology at Mercer University, secured approval from Mercer's institutional review board to conduct a survey of student sexual activity strikingly similar to the Mowrer-Meyer-DeGraff document. Dane asked the following:

How much of the time do you use contraceptives to prevent pregnancy?
(Please circle one.)
   a.) I/my partner almost always use(s) contraceptives during sexual activities.
   b.) I/my partner sometimes use(s) contraceptives during sexual activities.
   c.) I/my partner rarely use(s) contraceptives during sexual activities.

    d.) I/my partner never use(s) contraceptives during sexual
       activities.

How much of the time do you protect yourself from sexually
transmitted diseases?
  (Please circle one.)
    a.) I/my partner almost always use(s) protection during
       sexual activities.
    b.) I/my partner sometimes use(s) protection during sex-
       ual activities.
    c.) I/my partner rarely use(s) protection during sexual ac-
       tivities.
    d.) I/my partner never use(s) protection during sexual ac-
       tivities.

As at Missouri, the survey was developed in and was to be con-
ducted by Professor Dane's class, which was on research methods.
Mercer's president subsequently ordered the research stopped on
the ground, according to an extensive press account, that it
would offend students and parents. Professor Dane resigned.
Robin Wilson, *An Ill-Fated Sex Survey: At Mercer U., a Research
Project Sets Off a Debate over Academic Freedom,* Chron. Higher
Educ., Aug. 2, 2002, at A10.

   27. The literature is substantial. The issues are discussed in
Ethical Issues in Social Science Research (Tom Beauchamp et al.
eds., 1982) and Eleanor Singer & Felice Levine, *Protection of Human Subjects of Research: Recent Developments and Future
Prospects of the Social Sciences,* 67 Pub. Opinion Q. 148, 158
(2003). *See generally Improving the System for Protecting Human
Subjects: Counteracting IRB "Mission Creep,"* 13 Qualitative Inquiry 617 (2007).

   28. The question is currently under consideration by Committee A. *See Research on Human Subjects: Academic Freedom and
the Institutional Review Board,* Academe, Sept.–Oct. 2006, at 95
(subcommittee report published for public comment).

   29. *Committee on Academic Freedom: Statement on the Case
of Professor Louis Levine of the University of Montana,* 5 AAUP

Bull. 13 (1919). The chancellor advanced yet another ground for the exercise of his authority that is still encountered today. He argued that the published monograph identified Levine as "Professor of Economics in the Montana State University." (Inasmuch as the University of Montana was *the* state university, the names were apparently interchangeable.) The committee flatly rejected this argument:

Chancellor Elliott contended before the committee that this was not a private publication because Dr. Levine stated on the title that he was "Professor of Economics in the Montana State University." It is the custom of book publishers to place the title beneath the name of the author in practically all publications, and no one considers such publications as emanating from the universities to which the authors are attached. Because the author of a legal work describes himself as a member of the New York Bar, it does not follow that the work is to be understood as the work of the New York Bar Association. Works written by men who describe themselves as members of the Royal Society, National Geographic Society, or American Association for the Advancement of Science, are never understood by anyone to be official publications of those societies. If Dr. Levine had described himself as a former professor of some university such description would have had the same significance as the one used by him.

Id. at 23.

30. For example, when Florida Atlantic University sponsored a 2001 production of Terrence McNally's *Corpus Christi,* Florida's education commissioner, Charlie Crist, attacked the decision in a letter to the press. "How could administrators at F.A.U. have shown such poor judgment in spending taxpayers' money for this purpose? Reflexively, they cite 'academic freedom' as the rationale. Of course, 'academic freedom' is the final refuge in which professors hide when confronted with the absurdity and arrogance of their decisions. It is a wasteland entirely unmoored from standards, where any activity can be justified if it exceeds our 'comfort level' by 'challenging' our preconceptions." *Florida Of-*

ficial Slams University's Staging of Play He Calls an Attack on Christians, Chron. Higher Educ., Apr. 27, 2001, at A12.

31. *Academic Freedom and Tenure: Washington State College,* 23 AAUP Bull. 19, 21 (1937).

32. *Id.*

33. *Academic Freedom and Tenure: Mercy College,* 49 AAUP Bull. 245, 248, 250 (1963).

34. *Academic Freedom and Artistic Expression, reprinted in AAUP Policy Documents and Reports, supra* note 12, at 35.

35. In 1985, the Theater Department of Nassau Community College produced Christopher Durang's *Sister Mary Ignatius Explains It All for You.* The administration was subject to concerted attack in much the same way as Florida Atlantic University had been. *See supra* note 30. President Sean Fanelli defended the department even against efforts to have the college's budget reduced: "I believed from the outset that the production of this play by the theater department was a logical laboratory extension of the classroom experience. The public aspect of the presentation was, in fact, an essential ingredient for that student learning experience. For me the issue was not the satirical content of the play, but rather the issue of academic freedom. If I could cancel this play, I could cancel any play and I could censor the entire curriculum according to my personal views." Sean Fanelli, *Drawing Lines at Nassau Community College,* Academe, July–Aug. 1990, at 24, 24–25. President Fanelli was later awarded the AAUP's Alexander Meiklejohn Award for his defense of academic freedom in this case and in connection with subsequent attacks on course material that advocacy groups found offensive. Academe, July–Aug. 1995, at 57.

Chapter 4. Freedom of Teaching

1. Walter Metzger summarizes the attributes of *Lernfreiheit:*

Literally, *Lernfreiheit* meant "learning freedom" and in a bare decoding could signify no more than the absence of required courses. In Germany, it meant much more than that: it amounted to a disclaimer by the university of any control over the students' course of study save that which they needed to prepare them for state professional examinations or to qualify them for an academic teaching license. It also absolved the university of any responsibility for students' private conduct, provided they kept the peace and paid their bills. Having relegated general education to the gymnasium and residence halls to the crypt of history, the German university confronted its student body primarily as a purveyor of knowledge and as a credentializing agency, not as a parent surrogate or landlord. For their part, German students, obliged to find their own lodgings and diversions, liberated from course grades and classroom roll calls, free to move from place to place sampling academic wares, presented themselves to the university as mature and self-reliant beings, not as neophytes, tenants, or wards.

Walter P. Metzger, *Profession and Constitution: Two Definitions of Academic Freedom in America,* 66 Tex. L. Rev. 1265, 1270 (1988).

2. *AAUP Policy Documents and Reports* (10th ed. 2006), the so-called Red Book, contains the *Joint Statement on Rights and Freedoms of Students,* which was drafted in June 1967 by a committee composed of representatives from the AAUP, the United States National Student Association (now the United States Student Association), the Association of American Colleges (now the Association of American Colleges and Universities), the National Association of Student Personnel Administrators, and the National Association of Women Deans and Counselors. Each of these five sponsoring bodies has adopted the statement.

3. Hence Harvard president Abbott Lawrence Lowell: "Experience has proved, and probably no one would now deny, that knowledge can advance, or at least can advance most rapidly, only by means of an unfettered search for truth on the part of those who devote their lives to seeking it in their respective fields, and by complete freedom in imparting to their pupils the truth that they have found." Abbott Lawrence Lowell, *Report for 1916–17, quoted in* Henry Aaron Yeomans, *Abbott Lawrence Lowell, 1856–1943,* at 308–9 (1948).

4. Commission on Academic Freedom and Pre-College Education, *Liberty and Learning in the Schools* (1986).

5. The 1915 *Declaration* did not inherit the goal of empowering students to think for themselves from the German conception of university education. German practice focused far more on "'convincing' one's students . . . winning them over to the personal system and philosophical views of the professor." Richard Hofstadter & Walter P. Metzger, *The Development of Academic Freedom in the United States* 400 (1955).

6. Josiah Royce, *The Freedom of Teaching,* Overland Monthly, Dec. 1883, at 235, 237, 238. Royce anticipated the connection drawn in the 1915 *Declaration* between freedom and self-respect: "What scorn awaits the man that struts about as a genuine investigator, while all the time he knows that there are certain matters lying within his province that he dare not openly investigate, and may have to lie about. Yet such has been and is precisely the position of numerous teachers in places where the freedom of teaching has not come to be a recognized necessity. The very air of investigation is freedom." *Id.* at 238.

7. John Dewey, *Academic Freedom,* 23 Educ. Rev. 1, 8 (1902) (emphasis added) (quoting William Rainey Harper's 1900 presidential address at the University of Chicago).

8. *Academic Freedom and Tenure: Adelphi University,* 53 AAUP Bull. 278 (1967). The committee was chaired by R. K. Webb, a distinguished historian at Columbia University and later an editor of the *American Historical Review.*

9. *Id.* at 283.

10. We should note that the AAUP investigating committee nevertheless concluded that Krebs's conduct did not merit suspension, because it believed that Krebs had been given "good reason to think" that his methods of teaching were "perfectly acceptable." *Id.* at 284. "Testimony from members of the department is unanimous that there were no agreed decisions as to what should or should not be in the introductory course; no common syllabus was enforced. No doubt, in this extremely permissive atmosphere, Dr. Krebs fulfilled his role as gadfly, scourge, or mere eccentric in ways that were far from professional, as most academic scholars, in or out of the field of sociology, would interpret professionalism. But this raises the question of professional standards at Adelphi." *Id.* at 283–84. The committee thus considered

the examination an "error in judgment that should have been presumed remediable unless full proof of contumacy was established." *Id.* at 283. The committee noted that "if Dr. Krebs was incompetent by Adelphi standards, he was a probationer subject to perfectly simple and straightforward dealing: the University could have refused to renew his contract." *Id.* at 285.

11. We note in passing that were academic freedom to be reinterpreted as an individual right to transcend the discipline of professional norms, this distinction between indoctrination and education would be rendered unintelligible and the vulnerability of faculty to attacks for indoctrination would be correspondingly increased. See, for example, the organization NoIndoctrination.org, whose Web site may be found at http://www.noindoctrination.org (last visited Aug. 12, 2008), or the proposed Academic Bill of Rights, which may be found at http://studentsforacademicfreedom .org/documents/1925/abor.html (last visited Aug. 12, 2008).

12. Edward L. Thorndike, *The Teaching of Controversial Subjects* 1–2 (1937).

13. A. 4406, 2007–2008 Reg. Sess. (N.Y.) (as introduced in the Assembly, Feb. 2, 2007), *available at* http://assembly.state.ny.us/ leg/?bn=A04406&sh=t.

14. *Academic Freedom and Tenure: A Successfully Resolved Case at Northern Michigan University,* 55 AAUP Bull. 374 (1969). The report is captioned this way because the administration reversed itself and reappointed Professor McClellan with a raise in salary while the report was being prepared. The report was nevertheless published for its educational value, even as the association commended the university's president for his action.

15. Prior to distributing the petitions, Davis had secured the approval of both the acting chairman of his department and the dean of the college.

16. *Academic Freedom and Tenure: Arkansas Agricultural and Mechanical College,* 53 AAUP Bull. 385 (1967).

17. Is Your Professor Using the Classroom as a Platform for Political Agendas?, http://www.studentsforacademicfreedom.org /images/professor%20platform%20ad%20IN.pdf (last visited June 11, 2007).

18. *See* William McGuffrey Hepburn, *Academic Freedom and*

Tenure, 23 AAUP Bull. 642 (1937). The 1925 conference statement provided that "a teacher may not introduce into his class discussions controversial and irrelevant subjects outside his own field of study."

19. *Is a Scholar an Employee?,* New Republic, Mar. 11, 1925, at 57, 57–58.

20. Hepburn, *supra* note 18, at 649.

21. Conrad Russell, *Academic Freedom* 89 (1993).

22. In the nineteenth century, German professors employed a derisive term to describe students who attended the university for the sole purpose of career advancement, who had no deep commitment to *Wissenschaft* or *Bildung:* they were called *Brotstudenten*—literally "bread students." It had been commonly assumed that they were ignored by their professors, but more recent research indicates that German professors "often expressed a good deal of concern for the 'less gifted' students and adapted their pedagogical techniques accordingly." Arleen M. Tuchman, *Institutions and Disciplines: Recent Work on the History of German Science,* 69 J. Mod. Hist. 298, 303 (1997).

23. *Cf.* Cullen Murphy, *Are We Rome? The Fall of an Empire and the Fate of America* (2007).

24. *Cf.* Michael Rose, *How a Revolution Saved an Empire,* N.Y. Times, July 5, 2007, at A13.

25. *Academic Freedom and Tenure: University of Pittsburgh,* 21 AAUP Bull. 224, 247 (1935).

26. As the investigating committee noted, "The student testimony indicates that the work of the Survey Course did tend to make the students sympathetic with the lot of the common man and did make them feel that there was much which they, as active participants in the making of history, could do about it." *Id.* Turner's academic career was later pursued at Yale University after a period of federal government service.

27. *Academic Freedom and Tenure: State Teaches College (Murfreesboro, Tennessee),* 28 AAUP Bull. 662, 674 (1942).

28. *Academic Freedom and Tenure: Evansville College,* 35 AAUP Bull. 74, 91–92 (1949).

29. *Academic Freedom and Tenure: The Ohio State University,* 58 AAUP Bull. 306 (1972).

30. We do not mean to imply that Professor Green would have been out of bounds if he had adverted to and even discussed the national tragedy before proceeding to the assigned class syllabus; indeed, he might well have been thought callous by his students if he had not done so. We do not address here the question of whether faculty can cancel class—as an act of political protest, as an accommodation to student demands, or to prevent potential disruption—and what might be required by way of making up lost class time. This set of issues and attendant questions concerning the faculty's collective role in fashioning policy and in adjudicating alleged departures from institutional rules emerged in administrative reactions nationwide to class cancellations and "teach-ins" conducted in the wake of the killings at Kent State University and Jackson State College in 1970. *See generally Academic Freedom and Tenure: University of Missouri, Columbia,* 59 AAUP Bull. 34 (1973).

31. American Council of Trustees and Alumni (ACTA), *How Many Ward Churchills?* 38 (2006), *available at* https://www .goacta.org/publications/downloads/ChurchillFinal.pdf.

32. ACTA, *Intellectual Diversity: Time for Action* 2 (2005), *available at* https://www.goacta.org/publications/downloads/ IntellectualDiversityFinal.pdf.

33. Without distinguishing by sampling technique or how terms were defined, a rather crude self-reporting survey of faculty political orientation over time shows the following:

Faculty Political Persuasion

1969–1970*	2004–2005**
Left 5%	Far Left 7.9%
Liberal 41%	Liberal 43.4%
Middle-of-the-Road 27%	Middle-of-the-Road 29.2%
Moderately Conservative 25%	Conservative 18.8%
Strongly Conservative 3%	Far Right 0.7%

SOURCE: *Evertt Carl Ladd Jr. & Seymour Martin Lipset, *The Divided Academy* Table 2 at 26 (1975). **The Chronicle of Higher Education, Almanac 2006–07,* 28 (Aug. 23, 2006).

This leaves much to be explored and explained, not least what these categories might mean in the period 2004–2005 vis-à-vis what they might have meant in the period 1969–1970. As some of what was thought thirty years ago to be on the fringe of the political right has become mainstream today, surely one plausible reading of these figures is that the American professoriat has remained, politically, pretty much where it has been for almost two generations.

34. In 2006 the American Academy of Arts and Sciences passed the following resolution:

Statement of Principles

1. It is a clear violation of academic freedom to evaluate faculty or students based upon their political beliefs or affiliations.

2. The principle of academic freedom is at the very core of American higher education. It is the indispensable condition for colleges and universities that seek to expand the domain of knowledge. Academic freedom enables scholars, researchers, teachers, and students to pursue their curiosity in whatever direction it leads them. Academic freedom promotes scholarly competence and achievement; it establishes open intellectual inquiry; and it has produced the extraordinary insights and discoveries that are the hallmark of American higher education. Academic freedom fosters scholarly and scientific innovation by protecting those who challenge orthodoxies. It is the responsibility of college and university trustees, administrators, faculty, and students to respect, preserve, protect, and defend academic freedom.

3. Academic freedom requires, among other things, that individual faculty be evaluated by experts in their field based upon the quality of their scholarship, teaching, and institutional contributions. Academic freedom requires that this evaluation reflect both rigorous professional standards and the profound value of open intellectual inquiry.

4. The application of professional disciplinary standards by experts in the field allows ample room for intellectual debate within the academy; it is compatible with the robust expression of different perspectives. Although colleges and univer-

sities may properly seek a faculty of widely varying views, they may not pursue this goal by considering political beliefs or affiliations.

5. In the event that there is reason to believe that discrimination among faculty on the basis of their political beliefs or affiliations has occurred, the proper remedy is through procedures established by the institution for the protection of academic freedom. It is the responsibility of colleges and universities to have in place appropriate procedures to protect and preserve academic freedom, and it is the responsibility of administrators and faculty to implement these procedures in a fair and responsible manner.

American Academy of Arts and Sciences, *Statement on Academic Freedom, available at* http://www.amacad.org/projects/freedom.aspx (last visited Aug. 12, 2008).

35. David Hollinger, *What Does It Mean to Be "Balanced" in Academia?,* History News Network, Feb. 28, 2005, http://hnn.us/articles/10194.html. This formulation does not address the real but rare problem in which the bona fides of an entire department or discipline is attacked as "political." We have witnessed such attacks in the context of transdisciplinary programs like women's or ethnic studies. *See, e.g.,* David Horowitz, *No Ideologue Left Behind,* Weekly Standard, Nov. 12, 2007, *available at* http://www.weeklystandard.com/Content/Public/Articles/000/000/014/313rbeuw.asp. Such controversies put great stress on the ordinary functioning of a college or university, but the academic community is not without resources to respond. As David Hollinger explains, "It is the job of deans and provosts to keep abreast of . . . trans-disciplinary conversations, and to pressure particular departments and schools to change their way of doing things—to achieve, indeed, balance—if the parts of the learned world most qualified to judge are truly dubious about their research programs and their attendant teaching and public service activities." Hollinger, *supra.*

36. *See, e.g., Report on the University of Tennessee,* 10 AAUP Bull. 213 (1924). In 1923 Professor J. W. Sprowls was told by Pres-

ident Harcourt A. Morgan that he could not use James Harvey Robinson's *The Mind in the Making* in his course in adolescent psychology at the University of Tennessee, because of the book's discussion of evolution (an antievolution bill was then pending before the Tennessee legislature). Sprowls substituted a course dealing with a different subject matter because in his view a class on adolescent psychology could not be taught without reference to evolution. The subject matter of adolescent psychology was not taught at all.

37. Even when this narrow sense of balance is applicable, it in no way limits an instructor's freedom to communicate his or her studied view on professionally controverted questions. In 1860, for example, Louis Agassiz was free to communicate to his students his considered judgment of Darwin's theory, even though that view was later proved mistaken. Edward Lurie, *Louis Agassiz: A Life in Science* ch. 7 (1961). Today we would expect a physicist such as Lee Smolin to communicate to his class his own judgment of string theory, a judgment that may or may not be vindicated. Lee Smolin, *The Trouble with Physics: The Rise of String Theory, The Fall of Science, and What Comes Next* (2006). A half century ago, Maurice Ewing was free to teach his students his considered judgment of the theory of plate tectonics, even though Ewing later came to share in the scientific consensus that he had been incorrect. Ewing was one of the giants of physical oceanography and the founder of the Lamont Geological Observatory (now the Lamont-Doherty Earth Observatory) at Columbia University. He was a leading opponent of the theory of plate tectonics, although around 1966 he came to be persuaded by the theory because of the work of his students. Edward Bullard, *William Maurice Ewing*, 21 Biographical Memoirs of Fellows of the Royal Society 269, 288–89 (1975). (We are indebted to Professor Stephen Altaner for the reference.) Matthew Finkin studied geology under another opponent of the theory, worked as a research assistant at the Lamont Geological Observatory in 1965, and recalls the dispute with fondness. The controversy was so intense that Bullard reports Ewing having approached him just before the beginning of a conference on the subject with the words, "You don't believe all this rubbish do you?" *Id.*

38. ACTA, *supra* note 32, at 3, 9, 13.

39. National Association of Scholars, *A Response to the AAUP's Report, "Freedom in the Classroom,"* http://www.nas.org/polArticles.cfm?Doc_Id=32 (last visited Aug. 12, 2008).

40. This case is discussed in the introduction.

41. We do not now pause to address the difficult question of what it might mean to impose on faculty a duty to present alternative sides of politically controversial questions *fairly.* Need the positions of the Ku Klux Klan, the Communist Party, and the Church of the Brethren all be presented? On any question of political consequence there will likely be a pedagogically unmanageably large number of potentially competing views.

42. H.B. 04–1315, 64th Gen. Assem., 2d Reg. Sess. (Colo. 2004).

43. *Statement on Professional Ethics* (1966), *reprinted in AAUP Policy Documents and Reports, supra* note 2, at 171.

44. *Academic Freedom and Tenure: University of Pittsburgh, supra* note 25, at 243.

45. *Academic Freedom and Tenure: Indiana State University,* 56 AAUP Bull. 52, 53–54 (1970).

46. *Id.* at 54.

47. *Id.* at 55–56.

48. Mark Taylor, Op-Ed, *The Devoted Student,* N.Y. Times, Dec. 21, 2006, at A31. Taylor warns that "today, professors invite harassment or worse by including 'unacceptable' books on their syllabuses or by studying religious ideas and practices in ways deemed improper by religiously correct students."

49. Royce continued, "He [the instructor] knows not when he will be accused of wicked rebellion against established custom for having made use of a new way of teaching that seems to him the best possible way, or for having laid stress upon some part of his subject that tradition has been accustomed stupidly to neglect." Royce, *supra* note 6, at 239.

Chapter 5. Freedom of Intramural Expression

1. James McKeen Cattell, *University Control* (1913).

2. 1 C. B. Labatt, *Commentaries on the Law of Master and Servant* § 299, at 930 (2d ed. 1913).

3. *Id.* § 273, at 824.

4. *Id.* § 285, at 870–72. To place flesh on the bare bones of these legal rules, the case consistently cited by leading legal treatises of the period was the English decision *Lacy v. Osbaldiston* (1837) 8 Car. & P. 80, 173 Eng. Rep. 408, in which the manager of Covent Garden was dismissed for saying to a singer performing in the opera *Zampa,* "I wonder how you can perform in such rubbish."

5. James McKeen Cattell, *Academic Slavery,* 6 Sch. & Soc'y 421, 425 (1917).

6. 1915 *Declaration* (emphasis added).

7. Matthew Finkin, *Intramural Speech, Academic Freedom, and the First Amendment,* 66 Tex. L. Rev. 1323, 1335 (1988) (citations omitted).

8. *Report of the Committee of Inquiry on Conditions at the University of Utah,* 1 AAUP Bull. 1 (1915) [hereinafter *University of Utah Report*]. The investigating committee consisted of the chairman, Edwin R. A. Seligman (Columbia University); John Dewey (Columbia University); Frank A. Fetter (Princeton University); James P. Lichtenberger (University of Pennsylvania); Arthur O. Lovejoy (Johns Hopkins University); Roscoe Pound (Harvard University); and Howard C. Warren (Princeton University). Seligman, Fetter, and Lichtenberger represented the Joint Committee on Academic Freedom of the American Economic Association, the American Political Science Association, and the American Sociological Society. Warren represented the Committee on the Academic Status of Psychology of the American Psychological Association. After leaving Utah, Professor Knowlton went on to a long and distinguished career on the faculty of Reed College.

9. A private communication to Matthew Finkin from a student of this affair stated that Professor Knowlton, appearing in some matter before the board, had been asked by its chairman, who suffered from dyspepsia, what Knowlton professed and, upon being told that he was a physicist, the chairman inquired, in all seriousness, what "physic" Knowlton would recommend. Whence Professor Knowlton's private aside.

10. *University of Utah Report, supra* note 8.

11. Milton Derber, *The American Idea of Industrial Democracy, 1865–1965* (1970).

12. Samuel Harber, *Efficiency and Uplift: Scientific Management in the Progressive Era* 124–25 (1964).

13. 58 Cong. Rec. 40, 41 (1919).

14. *Report of the Committee of Inquiry on Conditions in Washburn College,* 7 AAUP Bull. 66, 68, 74, 83, 102, 106 (1921).

15. *Report on the University of Louisville,* 13 AAUP Bull. 429, 451–52 (1927). Gottschalk went on to a distinguished career at the University of Chicago.

16. *Academic Freedom and Tenure: Rollins College Report,* 19 AAUP Bull. 416, 422 (1933). Professor Rice eventually founded Black Mountain College.

17. Emphasis added.

18. The 1915 *Declaration*'s assertions were contested at the time. *See, e.g.,* Association of American Colleges, *Report of the Committee,* 53 Educ. Rev. 416 (1917).

19. *Academic Freedom and Tenure: Mount Mary College (South Dakota),* Academe, May–June 1999, at 51; *Academic Freedom and Tenure: North Greenville College (S.C.),* Academe, May–June 1993, at 54 [hereinafter *North Greenville College Report*]; *Academic Freedom and Tenure: Report of the Sub-Committee of Inquiry for William Jewell College,* 16 AAUP Bull. 226, 228 (1930) (questioning whether the president had misrepresented his credentials); *Report of the Sub-Committee of Inquiry for Colorado College,* 5 AAUP Bull. 51 (1919).

20. *Academic Freedom and Tenure: The University of Nevada,* 42 AAUP Bull. 530 (1956).

21. *Academic Freedom and Tenure: Johnson & Wales University (Rhode Island),* Academe, May–June 1999, at 46; *North Greenville College Report, supra* note 19.

22. *North Greenville College Report, supra* note 19; *Report of the Committee on the Dismissal of Professor Wells from Washington and Jefferson College,* 8 AAUP Bull. 53, 69 (1922).

23. *Academic Freedom and Tenure: Dean Junior College (Mass.),* Academe, May–June 1991, at 27; *North Greenville College Report, supra* note 19.

24. See, for example, the many Committee A cases addressing sanctions for releasing nonconfidential institutional information

to the press. *Academic Freedom and Tenure: Philander Smith College (Ark.),* Academe, Jan.–Feb. 2004, at 57 [hereinafter *Philander Smith College Report*] (*citing Academic Freedom and Tenure: Oklahoma State University,* 56 AAUP Bull. 72 [1970]); *Academic Freedom and Tenure: Tiffin University (Ohio),* Academe, Jan.–Feb. 2002, at 53; *Academic Freedom and Tenure: Wesley College (Delaware),* Academe, May–June 1992, at 24.

25. Harold Dodds, *Academic Freedom and the Academic President,* 28 Law & Contemp. Probs. 602, 602–3 (1963) (emphasis added).

26. *See, e.g.,* Matthew Finkin, *Disloyalty! Does* Jefferson Standard *Stalk Still?,* 28 Berkeley J. Emp. & Lab. L. 541 (2007).

27. Consider the recent events at Philander Smith College in Little Rock, Arkansas. President Trudie Kibbe Reed dismissed Professor Janice S. Chaparro for releasing nonconfidential information about the college's financial plans to the press without prior approval. President Reed remarked to the press, "'As a leader, just like all other CEOs, my authority cannot be challenged.'" *Philander Smith College Report,* supra note 24. Note the echo of J. Levering Jones's response to questions about Scott Nearing's dismissal in 1914, "No one has the right to question us." *See* chapter 2, note 7.

28. Efforts to censor faculty speech in order to protect the "bottom line" have assumed increasing significance as universities have become ever more entangled in relationships with business. For an illustration on how an institutional focus on finances can threaten academic freedom, see *Academic Freedom on Trial* 11 (W. Lee Hanson ed., 1998), which discusses a proposed university contract with a supplier of athletic equipment containing a "non-disparagement" clause that could potentially limit faculty criticism of the supplier or its contractors.

29. Consider the contractual requirement imposed on the faculty of Catawba College that they "support the administration." The AAUP investigating committee found that this requirement "may easily come into conflict with the *primary* responsibility of the faculty member to the institution, to his students, to society, and to the truth. Such a contractual commitment has no justifica-

tion in an academic institution." *Academic Freedom and Tenure: Catawba College,* 43 AAUP Bull. 196, 221 (1957) (emphasis added).

30. *E.g.,* Charles Dennison, *Faculty Rights and Obligations in Eight Liberal Arts Colleges* (1955).

31. *See generally* Henry L. Mason, *College and University Government* (Tulane Studies in Political Science, vol. 14, 1972). Mason quotes Ralph S. Brown of the Yale Law School to the effect that faculty participation in institutional government is a "'complement to the right and responsibility to teach conscientiously and to investigate freely.'" *Id.* at 55.

32. *Statement on Government of Colleges and Universities, reprinted in AAUP Policy Documents and Reports* 135 (10th ed. 2006). The statement was drafted by the AAUP, the American Council on Education, and the Association of Governing Boards of Universities and Colleges.

33. In an ironic twist, the U.S. Supreme Court held that faculty members of a private university who collectively possessed the right to recommend university policy were included within corporate management and thereby excluded from the coverage of the National Labor Relations Act. *NLRB v. Yeshiva University,* 444 U.S. 672 (1980). The Court noted that "traditional systems of collegiality . . . insulate the professor from some of the sanctions applied to an industrial manager who fails to adhere to company policy." *Id.* at 689. For criticism of the decision, see Matthew Finkin, *The* Yeshiva *Decision: A Somewhat Different View,* 7 J.C. & U.L. 321 (1980–1981). On the downright perversity of the Court's perception of where managerial control actually lay in Yeshiva University, see *Academic Freedom and Tenure: Yeshiva University,* Academe, Aug. 1981, at 186.

34. The limits of intramural expression have not been well charted in the AAUP's case law. Just as speech in the classroom is subject to limits, so is intramural expression. Attempts to physically silence a campus speaker out of disagreement with the speaker's views, even out of moral repulsion for the speaker, are not protected by academic freedom, no matter how sincere, deeply held, and principled the objection. *Northwestern University: A Case of Denial of Tenure,* Academe, May–June 1988, at 55.

Nor would serious criticisms of an administration be sheltered when uttered with knowledge of falsity. *Academic Freedom and Tenure: University of Cumberlands (Ky),* Academe, Mar.–Apr. 2005, at 99, 109; *Academic Freedom and Tenure: Wesley College (Delaware),* Academe, May–June 1992, at 24, 33.

Chapter 6. Freedom of Extramural Expression

1. *See Academic Freedom and Tenure: Indiana State University,* 56 AAUP Bull. 52 (1970); chapter 4, text accompanying note 45.

2. *See Academic Freedom and Tenure: The Ohio State University,* 58 AAUP Bull. 306 (1972); chapter 4, text accompanying note 29.

3. William Rainey Harper, *Presidential Address,* 5 U. Chi. Rec. 370, 377 (1901).

4. *Report on the University of Montana,* 10 AAUP Bull. 154, 158 (1924). The investigating committee included Ernst Freund of the University of Chicago Law School. The American Legion had attacked Professor Fisher's negative views on American involvement in the Great War.

5. The drafting of the 1940 *Statement's* protection for extramural utterance is recounted in Walter P. Metzger, *The 1940 Statement of Principles on Academic Freedom and Tenure,* 53 Law & Contemp. Probs. 3, 51–64 (1990), *reprinted in Freedom and Tenure in the Academy* 3, 51–64 (William Van Alstyne ed., 1993).

6. The interpretive comment was based on the *Committee A Statement on Extramural Utterances (1964), reprinted in AAUP Policy Documents and Reports* 32 (10th ed. 2006).

7. Arthur O. Lovejoy, *Academic Freedom, in Encyclopedia of the Social Sciences* 384, 386 (Edwin R. A. Seligman & Alvin Johnson eds., 1930).

8. Henry Aaron Yeomans, *Abbott Lawrence Lowell, 1856–1943,* at 310 (1948). John Searle makes a similar point, John R. Searle, *Two Concepts of Academic Freedom, in The Concept of Academic Freedom* 92 (Edmund L. Pincoffs ed., 1975), as does William Van Alstyne, William Van Alstyne, *The Specific Theory*

of Academic Freedom and the General Issue of Civil Liberty, in The Concept of Academic Freedom, supra, at 59. Most recently, the point has been made in Leslie Green, *Civil Disobedience and Academic Freedom,* 41 Osgoode Hall L.J. 381 (2003).

9. Rebecca Gose Lynch, *Pawns of the State or Priests of Democracy? Analyzing Professors' Academic Freedom Rights within the State's Managerial Realm,* 91 Calif. L. Rev. 1061 (2003).

10. *San Diego v. Roe,* 543 U.S. 77, 84 (2004); *see, e.g., Connick v. Myers,* 461 U.S. 138 (1983); *Pickering v. Bd. of Educ.,* 391 U.S. 563 (1968).

11. *See, e.g., Garcetti v. Ceballos,* 547 U.S. 410 (2006); *Urofsky v. Gilmore,* 216 F.3d 401 (4th Cir. 2000); *Bishop v. Aronov,* 926 F.2d 1066 (11th Cir. 1991); Ailsa W. Chang, *Resuscitating the Constitutional "Theory" of Academic Freedom: A Search for a Standard Beyond* Pickering *and* Connick, 53 Stan. L. Rev. 915 (2001).

12. *See, e.g.,* Noam Chomsky, *Hegemony or Survival: America's Quest for Global Dominance* (2003).

13. *Academic Freedom and Tenure at the Ohio State University,* 17 AAUP Bull. 443 (1931). Another ground given for Miller's dismissal was a press report that while in Korea—then a Japanese colony—Miller had been escorted out of a public lecture by Japanese authorities because in his remarks he had referred to Czechoslovakia as a "republic," a word whose utterance was forbidden by the Japanese.

14. Professor Miller's "laboratory practice" was to give interracial teas for students and to conduct class visits to historically black Wilberforce University. Class attendance was not obligatory for either, but even so the investigating committee quotes one trustee saying of Miller, "'He made his students dance with niggers.'" *Id.* at 454.

15. *Id.* at 445.

16. The consequences of justifying freedom of extramural expression in this way were made evident by John Silber when he was dean at the University of Texas. In 1967, in the heated environment of the Vietnam War, a young assistant professor of philosophy had asserted the existence of concentration camps (and a good deal more) in an impassioned political speech on the steps

of the Texas state capitol. Silber refused to renew the professor's appointment on the ground that he had "told a lie to make a rhetorical point." Silber believed that the professor had committed a "a gross betrayal of academic freedom." John Silber, *Poisoning the Wells of Academe,* 43 Encounter 30, 37 (1974). Silber is reported to have said to the philosopher that he couldn't be "a Socrates in Athens and a common sophist in the Piraeus." Ronnie Dugger, *Our Invaded Universities* 127 (1974). Silber's argument presupposes that protections for extramural speech derive from freedom of research and hence are subject to the professional standards that apply to freedom of research.

17. *N.Y. Times Co. v. Sullivan,* 376 U.S. 254, 270 (1964).

18. *See supra* note 8 and accompanying text.

19. *See Committee on Academic Freedom: Statement on the Case of Professor Louis Levine of the University of Montana,* 5 AAUP Bull. 13 (1919); chapter 3, text accompanying note 29.

20. *Academic Freedom and Tenure: Columbia College (Missouri),* 57 AAUP Bull. 513 (1971). The AAUP investigating committee deemed the repudiation of the employment agreement a violation of academic freedom because it "was based, in significant measure, not upon academic considerations but upon what was viewed as the public relations position of the College. The ad hoc committee does not consider this a proper basis of a decision of this kind. A decision so based essentially removes the authority for academic decisions from the faculty and administration to the community and thus seriously jeopardizes academic freedom, the exercise of which frequently results in community pressures." *Id.* at 517.

21. Yeomans, *supra* note 8, at 311–12.

22. *See Academic Freedom and Tenure: University of South Florida,* Academe, May–June 2003, at 59, 65–66.

23. *See Academic Freedom and Tenure: Evansville College,* 35 AAUP Bull. 74 (1949); chapter 4, text accompanying note 28.

24. *Id.* at 108 (emphasis added).

25. *Report of Committee A for 1947,* 34 AAUP Bull. 110, 126 (1948).

26. *Report of Committee A for 1948,* 35 AAUP Bull. 49, 60–61 (1949).

27. *Academic Freedom and Tenure: The University of Illinois,* 49 AAUP Bull. 25 (1963).

28. The committee concluded that the standard used by the University of Illinois to dismiss Professor Koch was inappropriate. The "concept of 'irresponsibility,'" the committee explained, "is exceedingly vague. Any one of us can easily call to mind statements by our colleagues which might be termed by some as unrestrained, undignified, or lacking respect for the opinion of others. Any serious application of the standard would tend to eliminate or discourage any colorful or forceful utterance. More likely, . . . the standard would be reserved as a sanction only for expression of unorthodox opinion." *Id.* at 37. Professor Emerson subsequently addressed the issue in Thomas Emerson & David Haber, *Academic Freedom of the Faculty Member as Citizen,* 28 L. & Contemp. Probs. 525 (1963).

29. *Academic Freedom and Tenure in the Quest for National Security,* 42 AAUP Bull. 49, 58 (1956). The report was supplemented by Committee A in 1958. *A Statement of the Committee on Academic Freedom and Tenure Supplementary to the 1956 Report, "Academic Freedom and Tenure in the Quest for National Security,"* 44 AAUP Bull. 3 (1958). The 1958 supplement reiterated this standard. *Id.* at 8.

30. There was a spirited dissent by one committee member, Warren Taylor (English, Oberlin College), and several other members of Committee A either did not vote or did not participate in the consideration of the case.

31. *Academic Freedom and Tenure: The University of California at Los Angeles,* 57 AAUP Bull. 382, 397 (1971) (emphasis added).

32. The point is illustrated by the action of the administration of the University of Colorado in the matter of Professor Ward Churchill. Professor Churchill had spoken crudely and disparagingly of the victims of the 9/11 terror attack in New York. Calls for his summary removal were resisted by the administration, which nevertheless appointed a committee to determine whether Professor Churchill's published work comported with scholarly standards. The committee concluded that his work was seriously derelict in several regards. *Report of the Investigative Committee*

of the Standing Committee on Research Misconduct at the University of Colorado at Boulder concerning Allegations of Academic Misconduct against Professor Ward Churchill (2006), *available at* http://www.colorado.edu/news/reports/churchill/download/WardChurchillReport.pdf. The administration took the committee report as a statement of charges that, if proved, would warrant serious discipline. It presented these before the university's faculty hearing committee, to which proceeding Professor Churchill was a party. The committee sustained some of the charges but was divided over the sanction to recommend. The president recommended that Professor Churchill be dismissed, and he was. Churchill's dismissal was predicated not on his extramural speech but rather upon the professional incompetence of his research. It is clear, however, that inquiry into the quality of Churchill's research would not have occurred but for the controversy stirred by his extramural speech. At the time of this writing, Professor Churchill is pursuing a case against the university in the courts.

Chapter 7. Conclusion

1. In 1932, there were 931 colleges and universities in the United States, of which 434 were religiously affiliated. Malcolm Willey et al., *Depression Recovery and Higher Education* 10 (1937). In 2005, there were 314 "faith-related" institutions in a universe of 4,387 institutions of higher education. Religiously affiliated institutions now represent just over 7 percent of all institutions of higher education. *Chronicle of Higher Education: The Almanac of Higher Education, 2006–7*, at 35 (2006).

2. For sharply contrasting contemporary views on the applicability of these ideals to church-related institutions, compare Michael W. McConnell, *Academic Freedom in Religious Colleges and Universities, in Freedom and Tenure in the Academy* 303 (William Van Alstyne ed., 1993), with Judith Jarvis Thomson & Matthew W. Finkin, *Freedom and Church-Related Higher Education: A Reply to Professor McConnell, in Freedom and Tenure in the Academy, supra,* at 419. For modern decisions involving controversy over ecclesiastical authority, see, for example, *Academic*

Freedom and Tenure: Brigham Young University, Academe, Sept.–Oct. 1997, at 52, and *Academic Freedom and Tenure: The Catholic University of America,* Academe, Sept.–Oct. 1989, at 27.

3. A recent controversy at the University of Illinois is a good illustration of this danger. *See Report of the Chancellor's Advisory Committee on the Academy on Capitalism and Limited Government Fund* (2007), *available at* http://www.senate.uiuc.edu/aclgf_report_of_advisory_committee.pdf.

4. Derek Bok, *Universities in the Marketplace: The Commercialization of Higher Education* (2003); *see also* the sources cited in chapter 3, note 12.

5. *See* chapter 6, text accompanying note 4.

6. *See* chapter 6, text accompanying notes 23–25.

7. *See* chapter 4, text accompanying notes 45–47.

8. This force can reach even private universities. A notable example occurred in 1935 when Charles Walgreen, the eponymous owner of the drugstore chain, removed his niece from the University of Chicago because she told him of "Communist influences" in the faculty. The Hearst press quickly sensationalized the episode, and the Illinois Senate reacted by investigating subversive activities in "certain tax exempt colleges and universities" in the state, namely, the University of Chicago. *See Report of the Special Committee Authorized by Senate Resolution No. 33,* J. Senate (Ill.), June 26, 1935, at 1304. The university was exonerated, and Mr. Walgreen later made a donation to it, presumably as a gesture of reconciliation. (Mr. Walgreen's niece, it seems, had sought to pull her uncle's beard.) Damage was nevertheless inflicted on faculty members named in the process as well as on the university. The episode is recounted by John Boyer, *Academic Freedom and the Modern University: The Experience of the University of Chicago* (2002).

9. *Committee on Academic Freedom: Statement on the Case of Professor Louis Levine of the University of Montana,* 5 AAUP Bull. 13, 24 (1919); *see also* chapter 3, text accompanying note 29.

10. *Academic Freedom and Tenure at the Ohio State University,* 17 AAUP Bull. 443, 446 (1931); *see also* chapter 6, text accompanying notes 13–15.

11. *Academic Freedom and Tenure: University of Pittsburgh,*

21 AAUP Bull. 224, 240 (1935); *see also* chapter 4, text accompanying notes 25–26.

12. *Academic Freedom and Tenure: University of Pittsburgh, supra* note 11, at 240.

13. *Academic Freedom and Tenure: Rocky Mountain College,* 42 AAUP Bull. 292, 303–4 (1956). It is not unknown for faculty themselves to abet outside groups in their public efforts to politicize what ought to be a purely internal and professional debate among scholars. *See* Christopher Jencks & David Riesman, *The Academic Revolution* 18 n.14 (1968).

14. Butler engineered the dismissal of James McKeen Cattell, whom Butler loathed, on trumped-up charges of disloyalty in wartime, despite Cattell's twenty-six years of service. Michael Rosenthal, *Nicolas Miraculous: The Amazing Career of the Redoubtable Dr. Nicholas Murray Butler* 226–35 (2006); *see also Columbia University v. Professor Cattell,* 8 AAUP Bull. 21 (1922) (reprinting some of the epistolary exchanges between Cattell, Butler, and the board of trustees). Charles Beard consequently resigned in disgust from the Columbia History Department. The incident may profitably be compared with Butler's refusal, six years later, "to interfere with Columbia University's assistant professor of Latin because the professor is a local head of the Fascisti movement." *Butler Won't Discipline Fascist Professor; Declares Columbia Is for Academic Freedom,* N.Y. Times, Apr. 9, 1923, at 1. Butler wrote the general secretary of the Italian Chamber of Commerce that "an individual whose personal acts tend to bring the university into contempt and to injure its influence may properly and without any departure from the highest university ideals be asked to carry on his work elsewhere. But to attempt to discipline a university teacher for his private or political opinions would be most unbecoming." *Id.*

15. Nicholas Murray Butler, *Academic Freedom,* 47 Educ. Rev. 291, 292, 294 (1914). Butler continued:

A gentleman measures his public utterance and bears himself with tolerance and kindliness toward those who are otherwise minded. A gentleman understands that it is neither necessary nor expedient to teach to the young everything which the experience and reflection of an older man may have taught him to believe. A gentleman has some appreciation of historic values and a sense of proportion. *He knows how to use the rich gift of freedom without divesting himself of a high sense of responsibility for that use.* The universities of the world, and, in particular, the leading universities of the United States, offer abundant illustrations of scholars who hold views on fundamental questions that are quite at variance with those in authority about them and who are yet as secure and as contented in their tenure of academic office as it is possible for men to be. They enjoy academic freedom, but they enjoy it like gentlemen. This is the crux of the whole matter.

Id. at 294 (emphasis added).

16. *Report of the Commission on Academic Freedom and Tenure of the Association of American Colleges* (1922), *reprinted in* 18 AAUP Bull. 376 (1932) (emphasis added).

17. It is true that the 1940 *Statement* itself asserts that in the context of extramural speech, faculty "should at all times be accurate, should exercise appropriate restraint, should show respect for the opinions of others, and should make every effort to indicate that they are not speaking for the institution." But appeals to standards of responsibility and restraint have not been confined to the context of extramural speech; nor did they begin with the 1940 *Statement;* nor have they abated after the 1940 *Statement* was authoritatively interpreted in 1970 to enact "the controlling principle . . . that a faculty member's expression of opinion as a citizen cannot constitute grounds for dismissal unless it clearly demonstrates the faculty member's unfitness for his or her position. Extramural utterances rarely bear upon the faculty member's fitness for the position." This reinterpretation is discussed in detail in chapter 6.

18. *Academic Freedom and Tenure: Evansville College,* 35 AAUP Bull. 74, 102 (1949); *see also* chapter 6, text accompanying notes 23–25; chapter 4, text accompanying note 28.

19. *Academic Freedom and Tenure: Indiana State University,* 56 AAUP Bull. 52, 55 (1970); *see also* chapter 4, text accompanying notes 45–47.

20. *Academic Freedom and Tenure: Alabama Polytechnic Institute*, 44 AAUP Bull. 158, 161 (1958). In an editorial, the school newspaper opined, "The Board is in favor of as much free speech as the financial security of the institution will permit." *Id.* at 165.

21. Israel on Campus Coalition, *Academic Rights, Academic Responsibilities: A New Approach* 7 (2007), *available at* http://www.israelcc.org/about/updates/academic_rights_responsibilities.htm. The report explains: "Professors should stand by colleagues whose academic freedom has been violated, but it is not in their interest to stand up automatically for every teacher who complains. *A faculty member who brings disrepute and outside scrutiny upon the academy does his colleagues no favors.*" *Id.* at 35 (emphasis added).

22. Fritz Machlup, *On Some Misconceptions Concerning Academic Freedom, reprinted in Academic Freedom and Tenure: A Handbook of the American Association of University Professors* 188, 191 (L. Joughin ed., 1969).

23. To require that faculty show "good judgment" and "restraint" as measured by the reactions of public opinion is to create a standard that is so vague that it cannot provide an ascertainable guide to speech or conduct. *See, e.g., Academic Freedom and Tenure: The University of South Florida*, 50 AAUP Bull. 44, 54 (1964).

24. Arthur O. Lovejoy, *Academic Freedom, in Encyclopedia of the Social Sciences* 384, 385 (Edwin R. A. Seligman & Alvin Johnson eds., 1930).

25. Machlup, *supra* note 22, at 188.

26. *See* John Henry Wigmore, *President's Report*, 2 AAUP Bull. 16 (1916).

Acknowledgments

We wish to express our deep appreciation to David Hollinger and Peter Novick for having read the manuscript and given so generously of their time and thought to provide trenchant criticism. We have benefited enormously from their help. We also wish to thank Stacey Ballmes for her unflagging assistance; our editor at Yale University Press, Michael O'Malley, for his goodwill and persistent support; and our copy editor, Karen Schoen, for her fine ear and her meticulous attention to detail.

Index

AAC. *See* Association of American Colleges

AAUP. *See* American Association of University Professors

abstract vs. concrete, 108–9

Academic Bill of Rights (Colo.), 192n.11

academic dissent, 61

academic expertise. *See* professional expertise

academic freedom: accountability and, 206n.24; American concept, development of, 1, 5–8, 30–52; American core principle of, 34; American current controversies over, 2–5; American standard of (see *Statement of Principles on Academic Freedom and Tenure*); American uniform meaning of, 52; artistic expression and, 74–77; codification and explication of, 6, 45–49, 142; constitutional law vs. professional understanding of, 8–9; contrasted with business and professional situations, 124; essential definition of, 7, 38–39, 44, 149; extramural speech in relation to, 132, 133–40, 143; faculty's status and, 114; four essential elements of, 7, 39, 157–58; German model of, 11, 18–19, 21–23, 30, 114; historical origins of, 6, 11–27; individual